Biopsychology

INTRODUCTORY PSYCHOLOGY

This series of titles is aimed at psychology students in sixth forms and further education colleges and at those wishing to obtain an overview of psychology. The books are easy to use, with comprehensive notes written in coherent language; clear flagging of key concepts; relevant and interesting illustrations; well-defined objectives and further reading sections to each chapter, and self-assessment questions at regular intervals throughout the text.

Published

INDIVIDUAL DIFFERENCES
Ann Birch and Sheila Hayward

DEVELOPMENTAL PSYCHOLOGY
Ann Birch and Tony Malim

BIOPSYCHOLOGY
Sheila Hayward

COGNITIVE PROCESSES
Tony Malim

COMPARATIVE PSYCHOLOGY
Tony Malim, Ann Birch and Sheila Hayward

RESEARCH METHODS AND STATISTICS
Tony Malim and Ann Birch

SOCIAL PSYCHOLOGY
Tony Malim and Ann Birch

PERSPECTIVES IN PSYCHOLOGY
Tony Malim, Ann Birch and Alison Wadeley

Series Standing Order

If you would like to receive future titles in this series as they are published, you can make use of our standing order facility. To place a standing order please contact your bookseller or, in case of difficulty, write to us at the address below with your name and address and the name of the series. Please state with which title you wish to begin your standing order. (If you live outside the United Kingdom we may not have the rights for your area, in which case we will forward your order to the publisher concerned.)

Customer Services Department, Macmillan Distribution Ltd
Houndmills, Basingstoke, Hampshire RG21 6XS, England

BIOPSYCHOLOGY
Physiological Psychology

Sheila Hayward

MACMILLAN

First published 1997 by
MACMILLAN PRESS LTD
Houndmills, Basingstoke, Hampshire RG21 6XS
and London
Companies and representatives
throughout the world

ISBN 0–333–64613–4

A catalogue record for this book is available
from the British Library.

10 9   8   7   6   5   4   3   2   1
06 05 04 03 02 01 00 99 98 97

Editing and origination by
Aardvark Editorial, Mendham, Suffolk

Printed in Hong Kong

Cartoons by Sally Artz

Contents

List of Figures

Preface

The aim of this book is to examine the relationships between the physiological mechanisms of the body, such as the sensory system, the nervous system and the endocrine system, and to see how these relate to mental processes such as those involved with perception, emotions, stress and biorhythms.

Chapter 1 discusses the reasons for studying physiology in conjunction with psychology, together with the methods of study used and the ethical basis for their usage. Information must first enter an organism before assimilation, learning or reactive behaviour can occur. This comes through one of the five senses: seeing, hearing, touch, taste, smell; therefore Chapter 2 looks at the human sensory systems. Chapters 3 and 4 examine the nervous and endocrine systems respectively, while Chapters 5–7 discuss the physiological and psychological interactions in areas such as emotion, motivation, stress and altered states of consciousness. Finally, readers are offered a glimpse into the future, as new methods of modelling the brain are outlined.

In line with other books in this series, the author has attempted to present material concisely, while giving as full an explanation as possible. It is hoped that the text may be used as an introduction to the area of physiological psychology, or as a revision text. Each chapter is prefaced by objectives to be met during that chapter, and each section within the chapter ends with some self-assessment questions, so that readers may test their own understanding of what has been read.

The independent student is advised to read through the text one section at a time and consider the questions at the end of each section. These may be reconsidered later, when the student has undertaken further reading. The aim of this book is to explain simply, one step at a time, so that nonbiologists will not feel disadvantaged.

While the books in this series are intended primarily for A level students, this particular volume is also likely to be useful to university undergraduates who are studying psychology, especially those without any science (biology/chemistry) background. In addition, students on nursing, BTec or social care courses may also find the book useful.

While 'introspection' is discouraged in many areas of psychology, the author here encourages readers to relate the phenomena described to their own personal physiological experiences, to try out demonstrations for themselves and to 'look and feel within their bodies', in order to become involved with the subject area under discussion.

To me, this is a fascinating area of study and one which I have always enjoyed teaching. I hope you will enjoy reading this book as much as I have enjoyed writing it.

Sheila Hayward

This book is dedicated to my students, past, present and future, especially my son, Robert, and my daughter, Emma.

Acknowledgements

The author and publishers wish to thank the following for permission to use copyright material:

Tom Cox for material from T. Cox, *Stress*, 1978, Figure 1.10 (p. 19); The *New England Journal of Medicine* for material from Kales and Kales, *The New England Journal of Medicine*, **290**, 1974, Figure 1 (pp. 487–99); Oxford University Press for material from J.A. Horne, *Why We Sleep; The Functions of Sleep in Humans and Other Mammals*, 1988.

Every effort has been made to trace all the copyright holders, but if any have been inadvertently overlooked the publishers will be pleased to make the necessary arrangement at the first opportunity.

He's never met her, but he says she has the
most beautiful brain scan and EEGs he's ever seen.

Introducing Biopsychology

1

By the end of this chapter you will be able to:

- discuss what is meant by the term 'physiological psychology';
- outline methods of study used in this area; and
- discuss the ethical constraints of research into physiological psychology.

SECTION I WHAT IS BIOPSYCHOLOGY?

Often also called 'physiological psychology', or occasionally 'psychobiology', this area explores the relationship between the mind and the body, and the interactive influence of one upon the other. As a simple example, if you have a cold (a physical virus infection), you may also feel that you have difficulty 'thinking straight', writing your psychology essays becomes exceedingly difficult! On the other hand, if you have a number of mental problems (exams looming, a quarrel with your mother or friend and your dog bit the postman), you may not undertake your usual work or physical activities with your usual gusto. This book aims to explore the mechanisms underlying these associations.

Two main areas of study of individuals include:

- **response mechanisms of the body**; and
- **the internal environment of the body**

and the **interaction** of these with the mind, the thought processes, memory and other higher functions.

Response mechanisms

The process of responding to incoming stimuli forms a chain of events, along the following lines:

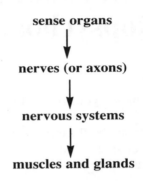

sense organs

nerves (or axons)

nervous systems

muscles and glands

used in making the appropriate responses.

These response systems are based in anatomy and physiology, the physical structure and functioning of the human body.

Internal environment

This includes a complex of substances within the individual's body:

- food materials;
- secretions of glands;
- metabolic products;
- blood and lymph constituents; and
- chemicals manufactured in the body and the brain.

The internal environment of the body involves biochemistry (the chemical substances involved in the body's structure and functioning) and endocrinology (the glands and hormones that influence these functions).

Why do we study biopsychology?

Human beings have always been curious to know how things work, and this extends to the workings of the human body. From this biological basis, it is a short step to enquire into the 'workings' of the brain, which does not function on a 'rods and pulleys' basis, but electrically and chemically. The question then arises as to whether the brain is synonymous with the mind and whether the mind controls the body.

This has been called the **mind/body question**. There are two different approaches to seeking answers:

- **Dualism** suggests that mind and body are separate: the body is matter but the mind transcends this. The two function independently. (Descartes, the eighteenth-century French philosopher, was a proponent of this view.)
- **Monism** believes that the universe, including the human body, consists of matter and energy, and that the mind is a product of the workings of the nervous system. Physiological psychologists take this approach and believe that empirical, practical investigations into the workings of the body, particularly the nervous system, will solve the mind/body problem and help to explain the relationship between input, thought processes and behaviour.

Although this philosophical debate was enjoyed for some time, this book will not devote a great deal of discussion to it, as it is obvious that, by definition, physiological psychologists see a mind/body relationship.

SECTION II   METHODS OF STUDY IN PHYSIOLOGICAL PSYCHOLOGY

In order to try to understand the relationship between the nervous system, the human body, thought processes and behaviour, psychologists have had to find methods of study that are not harmful to the individuals they are studying. So many of the processes involved are complex; they do not always seem to provide consistent results, because not all the variables can be controlled in a living human being. Currently, there are three main methods of study used in physiological psychology: the clinical method, the experimental method and scientific inference.

The clinical method

It would obviously be unethical to damage a person in order to examine the resultant loss of function, but people tend to suffer accidental damage from time to time. By careful examination of these individuals, it is possible to understand what physical damage has produced loss of which function. For example, stroke victims have provided a great deal of information for clinicians. A stroke results where a haemorrhage or a blockage of blood vessels has occurred in the brain. The result can be a blood clot that presses on the brain, preventing normal functioning of that area, or a deficit of blood to an area, which again prevents normal functioning. Early information from stroke patients showed that the left side of the brain controls the right side of the body and vice versa, for when the brain damage was on the left, paralysis occured on the right side of the body. In addition, right-sided paralysis was usually accompanied by loss of speech, which almost never occurred with left-sided paralysis. From this, we may deduce that speech is a function of the left side of the brain.

Accident victims from occupational, home or motor accidents often demonstrate loss of functioning that can be related to the degree or site of the head injury they have sustained. Before the compulsory introduction of motorbike helmets, thousands of young men contributed to this type of information; motorbike accidents inevitably caused head injuries, which could then be related to loss of function such as speech defects, paralysis and personality changes. Fortunately, this source of information is now much reduced.

Physiological damage is nowadays assessed by X-rays, electroencephlalograms (EEGs) and scans (see Figures 1.1 and 1.2), which are informative and provide cross-sectional pictures of brain areas.

1. *X-rays* show damage to solid structures, such as the cranium or skull, the bony casing of the brain.

FIGURE 1.1
CT scanner (for a description of this process, see Figure 1.4)

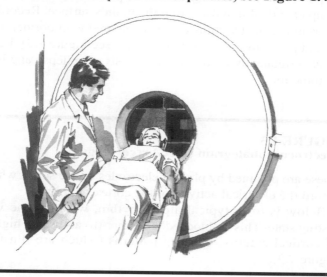

FIGURE 1.2
An image from a CT scan

The black and white image produced will show abnormalities in the brain, such as increased or reduced blood flow. PET and MRI scans produce coloured images, which give more information (see Box 1.1).

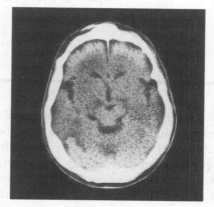

2. An *EEG* is a recording of the electrical activity of the cortex, or surface, of the brain. Electrodes are placed at specific points on the outer surface of the patient's skull; these pick up electrical impulses from the brain's surface. Recordings from accident victims can be compared with normal tracings, and problems detected in this way (see Figure 1.3). EEGs are also frequently used in the diagnosis of epilepsy and brain tumours.

FIGURE 1.3
Electroencephalogram (EEG) recordings

These are obtained by placing electrodes on the scalp, which then record the electrical activity of the cortex on a trace.

Below is (a) a typical alpha rhythm, which is the wakeful, resting state. This is 'blocked' by either (b) arousal, a higher level of cortical activity, or sleep patterns (which are illustrated in Figure 7.3).

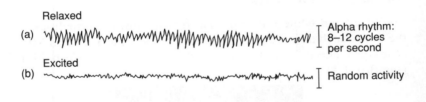

3. *Scans* (see descriptions below) give 'pictures' of the brain based on information of the metabolic functioning of certain areas (metabolic meaning the way in which the brain and the body use up fuel to produce energy for action).
4. *Psychological tests.* Loss of cognitive functioning is assessed by psychological tests, such as IQ tests, naming and memory

tasks and problem solving, which can be repeated from time to time in order to measure changes. The difficulty here is that there is no baseline measure of how well the individual funtioned in any particular way before the accident. Comparisons can only be made to norms established on a healthy population.

BOX 1.1 SCANNING TECHNIQUES USED IN DIAGNOSIS

CAT (or CT) scan

In **computerised axial tomography** (CAT), a moving beam of X-rays is passed across the patient's brain, in horizontal cross-section. The moving X-ray detector on the other side measures the amount of radioactivity that gets through, thereby detecting any difference in tissue density. The computer takes up this information and constructs a two-dimensional black and white image of the cross-section. Cross-sectional images of all areas of the patient's brain can be produced. This is known as a noninvasive technique, since it does not require surgery or the introduction of foreign substances into the patient's body.

PET scan

In **positron emission tomography** (PET), a substance used by the brain, for example glucose or oxygen, is tagged with a short-lived radioactive isotope and injected into the bloodstream. The radioactive molecules emit positrons, which are detected by the scanner. The computer analyses millions of these detections and converts them into a moving picture of the functioning brain, in horizontal cross-sections. These can be projected onto a colour screen; the metabolic rates of specific areas (where the tagged substance is being used more quickly) is indicated by a variety of specified colours on the screen. Moving pictures can indicate not only the sites of injury, tumours and nonactivity, but also the distribution in the brain of psychoactive drugs, and may indicate possible abnormal physiological processes in the brain. This is thought of as an invasive technique, because it involves introducing substances into the body.

MRI scan (sometimes called NMR scan)
Magnetic resonance imaging (or **nuclear magnetic resonance imaging**) is superior to CAT scans because it produces higher-quality pictures and therefore more information, yet does not require the invasive techniques of the PET scan. In MRI, the patient is placed inside a large circular magnet that causes the hydrogen atoms in the body to move. When the magnet is turned off, these revert to their original positions, producing an electromagnetic signal that is translated by the computer into pictures of brain tissue.

The experimental approach

The experimental approach to studying the nervous system is subject to keen ethical scrutiny. There are no problems with establishing test norms, for use as comparison data, as mentioned previously, but at the same time no risks of permanently damaging people can be taken; even seemingly simple experiments can prove disastrous. For example, in the 1960s some experiments were carried out to establish the location of the speech areas in the brain. Sodium amytal was introduced into the carotid artery, with the intention of temporarily inactivating the speech centre. Unfortunately, some participants did not recover their speech as expected. Nowadays, more stringent controls would ensure that any potentially dangerous experiment would be modified.

Scans or EEGs can be performed with intact, normal people, where input stimuli can be varied and the resultant changes in the responses on the traces or the screen can be noted. These can be used for comparison with clinical patients.

Drugs and experimental surgery are always piloted on animals first. There are, of course, objections to this: ethical objections include those of using animals as experimental objects at all, although in fact the animal species may also benefit from one's findings. (If no animal experiments were ever carried out, vets would still be groping in the dark!) In addition, there is the objection that human nervous systems are far more complex than those of animals, so any findings will be of limited value; however, in a dark space, even a glimmer of light is helpful to point the way. Much of the knowledge of basic physiology, such as that of the eye, instanced in Chapter 2, stems from findings in animals and has benefitted both animals and humans. Animal experiments are now subject to a stringent code of ethics and must avoid any unnecessary pain and suffering to the animal. (Ethics is discussed in the next section.)

Scientific inference

While it would not be scientifically acceptable to generalise from a clinical or experimental sample of one individual to the whole population, it is possible to make inferences from a number of patients suffering similar damage and functional deficits, or from batches of experimental data providing similar findings. Information that points the way to a hypothesis can be substantiated by further clinical trials or controlled experiments, and sound conclusions drawn. Scientific inference is based on known occurrences but looks forward to an overall picture.

SECTION III   AREAS AND APPROACHES TO PSYCHOLOGY

Is psychology not just one subject?

As with the detailed study of most things, separate subject areas are identified for convenience and ease of study. The same happens with psychology: areas of study are identified so that these can be examined in detail, and then integrated into the whole which is psychology, the study of human beings and their behaviour. There are five major approaches to the study of psychology: **physiological**, **psychoanalytical**, **behaviourist**, **cognitive** and **humanistic**. They are complementary areas of study, and there is often overlap between them and different ways of viewing the same problem.

The physiological approach is the area of study introduced by this book. It looks at the relationship between the physiological functions of the body and their relationship to mental activity and human behaviour. Earlier in this chapter, the **mind/body question** was referred to: whether the mind and the body are totally separate or whether the functioning of one is inextricably linked with the other. The idea that all psychological phenomena can be explained by physiological processes is termed **reductionism**: explanations are 'reduced to' the level of the smallest components. In physiological terms, this would involve analysis of biochemical activity, and nervous system and muscle processes. This may seem an extreme viewpoint and is not necessarily held by all physiological psychologists. Physiological processes may underpin a great deal of human behaviour but do not always provide satisfactory explanations for concepts such as the exercise of free will, facets of personality and other intangibles.

The **psychoanalytical approach** is based on the work of Freud and holds that human behaviour is influenced by the unconscious mind. Therapy involves uncovering what is in the unconscious, in order to resolve problems at source. This differs from the **behaviourist approach**, which regards overt behaviour as the expression of mental activity; behavioural therapies aim to change aberrant behaviours rather than enquire into possible causes. These changes are brought about by encouraging appropriate behaviours by **reinforcement** (a reward system appropriate to that individual). Nowadays, these therapies often incorporate **cognitive mediators**, examining and if necessary restructuring the thought patterns preceding abnormal actions. This, of course, is linked to the cognitive approach to psychology.

The **cognitive approach** involves investigation into the individual's thought and memory processes. The human mind is often compared with a computer, and people are seen as **information processors**. Some of the more informational models of the brain have been produced in this way (see next section), bringing forward a whole new area called **cognitive science**, amalgamating traditional cognitive approaches with leading-edge information technology. Findings from this feed back into the area of physiological psychology, which demonstrates nicely that all areas of psychology are not distinct entities but are interlinked and interdependent.

The **humanistic** (or **phenomenological**) **approach** regards all human beings as distinct individuals, with the potential for growth and fulfillment. They emphasise the need for self-esteem in humans, which is unrecognised in the more mechanistic approaches to psychology. It is important to remember that, while a cockroach has a brain (and possibly a 'mind') that instructs its physical activity, it has, as far as is known, no need for self-esteem. This serves to underline the concept that humans are 'more than the sum of their parts', but the functioning of those parts may provide the baseline for higher aspirations.

Ethics

The British Psychological Society has a strict code of ethics, which must be applied in all areas of psychology: investigations, experimentation and treatment. Some areas of physiological psychology would also be subject to General Medical Council guidelines. Two important areas covered are **risks** and **informed consent**.

The most obvious form of risk is that a participant might experience some form of **distress**, such as fear, anxiety, stress, guilt or loss of self-esteem. Psychologists have an ethical obligation to avoid causing these, even if it means abandoning a research project. Participants must not be asked to run **physical risks**, by either performing dangerous tasks or ingesting potentially harmful substances. Some of the studies and experiments that were carried out in the past would not now be allowed by an ethics committee.

Participants must not be subject to **coercion**, either to participate in a study in the first place or to continue with a study if they express a desire to leave before the end. **Confidentiality** must be observed by the psychologist: findings about individual participants may not be revealed without their express permission. **Privacy** is an entitlement of everyone; in observation studies, people must not be 'spied upon' but may only be observed in public places.

Informed consent must be obtained from all participants and patients; in the case of children, permission from their parents or guardians must be obtained. **Deception** should be avoided; if a study would be negated by giving full information to participants, for example in a study where comparisons were to be made between 'knowing' and 'not knowing' conditions, researchers should carry out a pilot study and interview participants afterwards to find out whether procedures were found to be acceptable.

Physiological and psychological knowledge could not advance without a certain amount of risk, but this must be minimised in the pursuit of the goals of preventing psychological problems.

Research with animals

This is a highly emotive subject and one which is argued strongly on both sides, by those for and those against the use of animals in research. Research is now governed by the Animals (Scientific Procedures) Act 1986, which protects living vertebrates.

The proponents of involving animals in experiments say that, if Darwin's theory holds, all species are related to each other through evolution; therefore, findings from animal experiments will indicate potential answers in humans. Studies that involve, for example, controlled breeding programmes could not be carried out with humans, not only because of the length of time it takes to produce several generations of humans, but also because it would be wrong both socially and ethically to design a human breeding programme. (Adolf Hitler was the last person to try to organise that!) With domestic and farmed animals, breeding is normally controlled by humans, and this does not seem to raise ethical questions.

As animals are less complex than humans, their systems can be understood more easily. If you were trying to understand mathematics, you would probably start with simple arithmetic rather than differential calculus. In the same way, the nervous system of a vertebrate lower down the phylogenetic scale (the evolutionary order of species development) provides a more sensible starting point than does the human nervous system. However, it can then be argued that their very differences can confuse research, because of **species-specific** differences.

Current legislation insists that animal experiments should be approved first and should inflict no, or only minimal, suffering on the animals concerned. Operations should not be carried out without anaesthetics. Certainly in the past, and the same will probably be true of the future, findings from animal experiments have been of enormous benefit, not only to humans, but to animals as well.

SECTION IV MODELS OF THE NERVOUS SYSTEM

From the base of scientific inference, models have been proposed. **Cognitive models** suggest how the human cognitive processes, such as perception, memory and thinking, are integrated and interact to provide the functioning of the individual.

Artificial intelligence (AI) modelling tries to provide a parallel between the human brain and the computer; initially, there were problems with this comparison, because computers used serial processing (processing one item after another, albeit very quickly) in a specific sequence, whereas the human brain uses parallel processing (it can draw in seemingly irrelevant information into its computations and process more than one string at a time). Now computers are available that can use parallel processing and even 'create' their own new information, using material already available to them. Designing ways in which they can do this has given scientists insight into potential ways in which the human brain may be doing the same thing. When an idea or answer comes to you 'out of the blue', it may be that your brain has been processing numerous bits of information without your being aware of it; only the answer reached your conscious mind. Connectionist models suggest that, potentially, all areas may be in contact with all other areas, making a network rather than a linear sequence of processing. Each of the 'cells' in the net represents neurones in the nervous system – these are described in Chapter 3, Section I.

SUMMARY

Physiological psychology investigates the mind/body relationship, on the grounds that the two are inextricably linked. Research evidence, rather than philosophical discussion, has led to this assumption.

There are several sources of information available to psychologists and physiologists. Clinical data from victims of accidents or other trauma can be compiled, using up-to-date investigation methods such as scans. Tests can be used with clinical patients and their results compared with the patients' functioning at a later date or after treatment. If these results are compared with those of the general population, scientific inference is used to determine what type of behavioural deficit is due to the trauma suffered. Information from animal studies has been extremely useful in contributing knowledge and suggesting areas for investigation, but humans are, of course, far more complex than other species, both structurally and behaviourally. Artificial intelligence models, using computer-generated information, are attempting to cast light on the integrated functioning of the brain and its influence on the individual.

SELF-ASSESSMENT QUESTIONS

1. What is meant by the term 'physiological psychology'?
2. Why do psychologists spend more time studying the brain than the body?
3. Compare and contrast three types of scan used in clinical investigations of brain function.
4. Describe how scientists use 'scientific inference' in physiological psychology.
5. What ethical problems must physiological psychologists consider?
6. What are the arguments for and against the use of animals in experiments?

Some visual system! Only two eyes, and those both facing the _SAME WAY_!

Sensory Systems   2

By the end of this chapter you will be able to:

- understand the basis of how humans receive input through the five senses;
- be familiar with the human visual system, from eye to brain;
- understand the relationship between the visual system and perception;
- have a working knowledge of the auditory system; and
- understand basic concepts relating to smell, taste, touch and kinaesthetic feedback.

INTRODUCTION

Perception is a process of the brain making sense of the input from the modalities. Gregory (1966) suggests:

> Perception is not simply determined by stimulus patterns; rather it is a dynamic searching for the best interpretation of the available data.

Sensation, therefore is the primary process of data collection from the environment. Perception is the secondary process of interpreting these data; the brain may add to the sensory input from memory or try to rationalise what it believes it should be seeing. Where information is ambiguous, the brain comes to the best solution it can (see Figure 2.1).

FIGURE 2.1
The Necker Cube

Is the dot on the front face or the back of the cube? Keep watching, and the dot will appear to change from front to back of the cube as your brain searches for the best possible interpretation to avoid ambiguity.

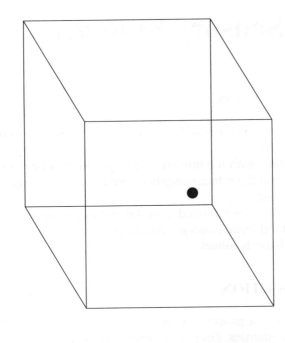

The physiological basis of perception is specific to each of the senses, or modalities. Each sense has receptors designed for its own specific job. If your eyes are injured and can no longer be used for seeing, your hearing may become more acute to compensate, but you cannot use your ears for 'seeing' because the mechanisms of action are totally different. The phenomenon known as **blindsight** (see Box 2.1) appears to be related to consciousness rather than vision.

Humans are highly visually oriented beings; at least 80 per cent of our input comes through our visual system, and the next largest percentage through our auditory system, with the other three modalities sharing the remaining few per cent. The priorities in this chapter are therefore similar.

Box 2.1   *BLINDSIGHT*

Damage to one side of the visual cortex produces a loss of vision in the visual field on the opposite side, or total loss of vision if damage involves all of the visual cortex. Weiskrantz (1987; Weiskrantz *et al.*, 1974) found that if an object is placed in a patient's blind field and the person is asked to reach for it, he or she will be able to do so accurately. The patient even opens his or her hand wider when a larger object is presented. Patients are surprised when their hand contacts the object.

This phenomenon shows that visual information can control resultant movements, without conscious awareness of visual sensation. The physiological mechanisms that make this possible are not wholly understood, but an essential link seems to be intact connections between two adjacent subcortical areas, the superior colliculi and the lateral geniculate bodies (these areas are described later in this chapter).

SECTION I   THE VISUAL SYSTEM

The eye

The **eye** is the first-line recipient of incoming visual stimuli; therefore, it is necessary to know a little about its structure and functioning.

Light rays from objects in the visual field enter the eye through the **lens**, which changes shape in order to focus these light rays onto the **retina**, at the back of the eye, to provide a sharp image. If we say that people are shortsighted or longsighted, what we usually mean is that the lens cannot **accommodate** enough (shorten or stretch) to provide a clear image. This is why sight usually gets worse as people get older: the lens and its controlling muscles are not working as well as they did when they were younger.

The **pupil** of the eye (effectively, the opening in the coloured **iris**) controls the amount of light entering the eye; in bright sunlight it contracts, and in dim lighting it dilates, or opens, to let in the maximum light possible. There are other reasons for pupils

FIGURE 2.2.
Diagram of the eye

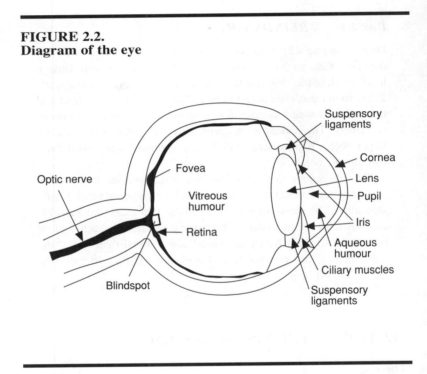

dilating: if we are very interested in something, or if we are afraid or disturbed, or under the influence of certain drugs, our pupils will dilate even in bright light. The pupils are not under conscious control but are controlled by the **autonomic nervous system**, which is described in Chapter 3.

The **retina** is the inner surface at the back of the eyeball. The **image** on the retina is upside down (see Figure 2.3) due to the crossover of light rays through the lens, as with a camera, focussing light onto a film.

FIGURE 2.3
Visual stimulus and retinal image

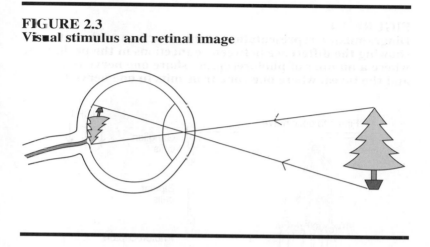

You do not perceive objects as being upside down because the brain 'turns' them the right way again; this is one of the differences between seeing and perceiving. **Seeing** is the physical process involved in vision, whereas **perceiving** is what the brain does with the incoming visual information. This is discussed more fully in *Cognitive Processes*, by Tony Malim, in this series.

The retina

The retina consists of a layer of light-sensitive cells called **photoreceptors**. There are two main types of these: rods and cones. **Rods** function best in dim light, are sensitive to movement but are not sensitive to colour; there are approximately 120 million rods in each human retina. Although there are fewer **cones** (about 6 million), they provide most of our visual information Cones are colour sensitive, function mainly in bright light and are concentrated mainly in the centre of the retina, to provide high **visual acuity**. This is the ability to see details sharply; the visual acuity of a hawk, for example, is far greater than that of a human. The hawk can spot a mouse at 500 metres, whereas a human cannot; each is specialised to what is important to it. The area of highest visual acuity on the retina is called the **fovea**, which consists almost entirely of cones.

FIGURE 2.4
**Diagrammatic representation of the structure of the retina,
showing the difference between connections in the periphery,
where a number of photoreceptors share one nerve fibre,
and the fovea, where one cone transmits to one nerve fibre.**

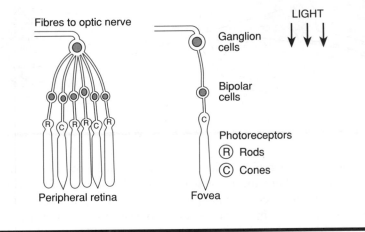

The retina appears to have been put on 'inside out'. The nerve
fibres (or **axons**) leaving the rods and cones transmit visual information to the brain, actually travelling across the surface of the
retina. These link into **bipolar cells** and **ganglion cells** (see
Figure 2.4), which are also on the surface of the retina, in addition to the blood vessels that serve the area. However, this does
not seem to interfere with the quality of information picked up
and transmitted by the retina. The only place where information
is not registered is the **blindspot**. This is where the nerve fibres
from the photoreceptors collect together and form the commencement of the **optic nerve**. We are not usually aware of a 'gap' in
our vision caused by the blindspot, because of two things: (a) the
brain compensates and fills the gap for us, and (b) we have two
eyes; it is unlikely that the same 'bit' of visual input would hit the
blindspot of both eyes.

If you would like to find your own blindspot, cover one eye,
focus on the square in Figure 2.5 and move the page slowly away

from you or towards you, still focussing on the square. The circle will suddenly 'disappear'.

Functions of the retinal cells

Rods

Rods are situated mainly at the periphery of the human retina. As they are sensitive to **movement**, this assists you to see a potential predator creeping up from the side. How often have you said, 'I saw something move out the corner of my eye'? You are aware of the movement before you have identified what the moving object is.

Another function the rods perform is to enable you to see in dim light. When you go into a dark room, away from bright light, you initially feel that you cannot see a thing! After a few seconds, vague shapes are discernible, and after approximately seven seconds, you are coping reasonably well. This is called **dark adaptation** and represents the length of time it takes for the rods to take over vision from the cones. Colours are not recognised by the rods, hence the saying 'all cats are grey in the dark'!

Cones

As mentioned earlier, cones are responsible for vision in bright light and provide for high visual acuity. Both rods and cones have nerve fibres that connect into a reduction system of bipolar cells and then to ganglion cells. As Figure 2.4 above shows, many receptors ultimately share one axon, except in the fovea, where there is a one-to-one relationship between photoreceptor cells and axons. Messages from this area obviously take priority.

Colour vision

Cones are also thought to be responsible for **colour vision**. There are a number of different theories of how we see in colour.

Trichromatic theory

First proposed in the nineteenth century by von Helmholtz (1885), trichromatic theory suggests that there are three types of cone,

---

FIGURE 2.5
Find your blindspot

Cover one eye. Focus on the square. Move the page slowly towards or away from you, still focusing on the square. Suddenly the circle will 'disappear'.

■   ●

---

each being sensitive to light of a particular wavelength: red, green or blue (see Figure 2.6). The perception of colour is due to the integration of information by the brain, from information provided by these receptors. This theory is supported by findings from studies of colour blindness, in which deficits in one or more colour receptors show a lack of perception of the related colours. This cannot be the whole story, of course, as the theory does not satisfactorily explain how we see bronze, for example. This may well be due to an interaction of innate colour-recognition processes and learned concepts, such as 'shiny' or 'metallic'.

FIGURE 2.6
Rods, cones and wavelengths of light

This shows the wavelengths that transmit the colours blue, green and red. Where these 'overlap', we see 'mixed' colours: yellow, orange, and so on. Rods transmit their information as black/white/shades of grey, as they function in dim lighting.

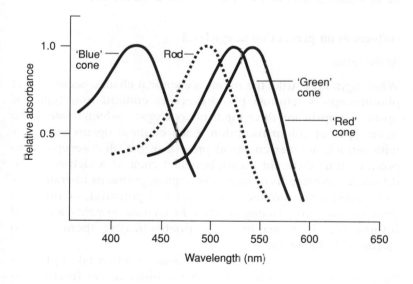

Opponent process theory

Colour perception is very much a subjective experience. Hering (1878) observed that people never reported seeing 'yellowish-blue' or 'reddish-green'. This led him to propose that red–green and yellow–blue perceptions were separate and opponent processes. This has been supported by later physiological findings that demonstrate **colour-opponent cells** in the retina (Svaetichin, 1956) and in the **lateral geniculate bodies** (DeValois and Jacobs, 1984; DeValois and DeValois, 1988). A third factor, the perception of **luminance**, is also necessary for a complete description of colour coding. This, it has been suggested, can be regarded as the proportion of red, green and blue recognised in the perception of any one colour.

These two theories, trichromatic theory and opponent process theory, are not necessarily irreconcilable. Hurvich (1981) suggests a two-stage colour theory that combines both theories. The three types of colour receptor of trichromatic theory may stimulate the appropriate colour-opponent cells for their wavelength, while inhibiting the inappropriate colour-opponent cells. The output from these would determine the resultant colour perceived.

Influences on perception at eye level

At the retina

When light rays strike the retina, a chemical change occurs in the photoreceptors. Human photoreceptors contain four types of opsin: rod opsin and three kinds of cone opsin, which relate to the three types of colour reception. Each of these opsins combines with retinol, another chemical present in the photoreceptors, to produce four different photopigments, each of which reacts to different wavelengths of light. These photopigments liberate electrical energy that produces the electrical potential, or impulse, which is transmitted along an axon. From now onwards, all visual information is transmitted electrochemically; there are no 'pictures' in the brain.

It is possible that some form of visual selection takes place in the retina, selecting information that is important or filtering out information that is less important. Hartline (1938) demonstrated that this happens with frogs; there are specific cells in the frog retina (crucial to survival) that act as 'bug detectors', and others which fire when the creature's horizon darkens, warning of the possible approach of a predator. Human equivalents of these have not been found because of the problems of experimenting with human eyes; however, we have recognised that rods respond to movement and cones differentially to colours.

Monocular influences

In order to focus on objects, the lens changes shape, pulled by the ciliary muscles. Information from **kinaesthetic receptors** in these muscles is fed back into the brain, giving **primary spatial information** about the object (where it is located in space) and information about the **accommodation** of the eye, that is to say, the amount it has had to change in order to focus on the object it is looking at.

Binocular influences

We normally use both eyes for focussing on objects, and the eyes are turned or **converged** to focus on the object. Feedback from **kinaesthetic receptors** in these muscles is integrated with the information on accommodation to confirm the spatial arrangement of objects in the visual field.

Self-assessment questions

1. Describe how rods, cones and axons transmit visual information.
2. How do we see colour? (Compare opponent process and trichromat theories.)
3. What are the effects on visual perception of (a) monocular influences, (b) binocular influences?

SECTION II   VISUAL PATHWAYS AND PERCEPTION

From the retina, visual information is electrically coded and passed along individual axons to **bipolar cells** (see Figure 2.4 above), then on to **ganglion cells**, where information may be combined (except for cells in the **fovea**, as we have already mentioned, where each has one-to-one cell-to-axon representation). Axons then ascend towards the brain via the optic nerve.

Information from each eye crosses over at the **optic chiasma**, so that there is an overlap of information from each eye transmitted onwards to the brain (see Figure 2.7). Both optic tracts then continue to the **lateral geniculate bodies**, situated in the thalamus, one of the subcortical structures of the brain. Each optic tract then relays information onwards to the **visual cortex**, the part of the brain that recognises and deals with visual information. It also sends information to other areas of the brain that incorporate visual information into their main activities.

The visual cortex is situated at the back of the brain. As you can imagine, dealing with such complex and voluminous information as visual input, scientists are still unravelling many of its complexities. We shall only mention a few of their findings to date.

Hubel and Wiesel (1979; Hubel, 1977) discovered that **neurones** (brain cells) in the visual cortex responded selectively to specific features of the visual world. They initially identified two kinds of cells: simple cells, which only responded to one stimulus, and complex cells, which would respond to a specific range of stimuli and movement of those stimuli. Other neurones were not sensitive to features such as the slope of lines, but were sensitive to, for example, colour (Livingstone and Hubel, 1987). Blakemore (Blakemore and Cooper,1977) found that kittens who had been deprived of specific visual stimuli from birth were later unable to respond to those stimuli; their neurones had either atrophied or possibly been commandeered for other purposes by the brain.

These experiments, and many others, demonstrate that even before birth brain cells are already specialised for a specific purpose, not only as 'visual' cells but also for a particular role within that system.

FIGURE 2.7
Visual pathways in the brain

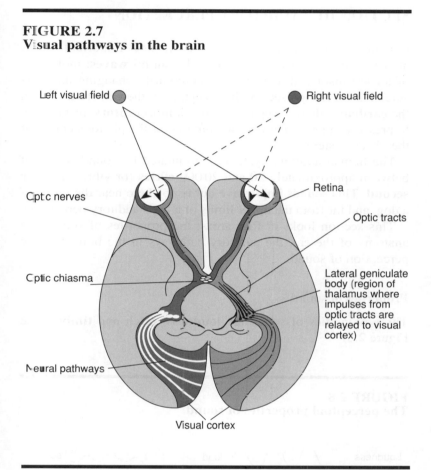

Self-assessment questions

1. Draw a diagram of the visual pathways from the eye to the visual cortex.
2. What occurs at the optic chiasma? What is the result of this?
3. How is visual information represented in the cortex?
   (A description and discussion of the work of Hubel and Wiesel, Livingstone and Hubel, and Blakemore, is relevant here.)

SECTION III   AUDITORY PERCEPTION

For most people, hearing is the second most important sense, after vision. Sounds are transmitted by **sound waves**; molecules of air are displaced and reform, temporarily changing air pressure. This is recognised by the receptors in the ear, starting with the **eardrum**; these receptors are **mechanoreceptors**, responding to pressure, a process different from that of the photoreceptors of the visual system.

The human auditory system is stimulated by sound waves of between approximately 30 and 20 000 **cycles** (or vibrations) **per second**. This sounds impressive but is nowhere near the range of a dog, and far from the upper limits of a bat's auditory perception.

This section looks at four areas: the properties of sound, the anatomy of the ear, the auditory pathways in the brain and the perception of sound.

Properties of sound

Three properties of sound are **loudness**, **pitch** and **timbre** (see Figure 2.8)

FIGURE 2.8
The perceptual properties of sound

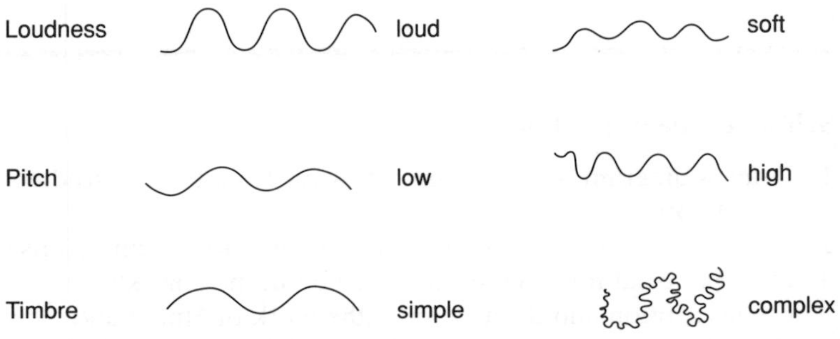

Loudness	loud	soft
Pitch	low	high
Timbre	simple	complex

Loudness

More vigorous vibrations produce greater air displacement and pressure, and this is recognised by the auditory system as loudness. Because the receptors within the ear (which we will look at in a moment) have to move to respond to loudness, a very high volume causes the perception of physical pain. Sustained loudness can damage the receptors.

Pitch

This we have already mentioned in the introduction. It is the frequency of vibration of the sound waves. It is measured in cycles per second or **hertz**, after the nineteenth-century scientist who discovered this property of sound.

Timbre

Timbre is the nature of a sound, whether it is the sound of a car engine or a person talking. Sounds that occur naturally are **complex**, containing more than one frequency of vibration; the resultant mixture determines the sound's timbre.

The anatomy of the ear

Figure 2.9 gives a diagrammatic representation of the outer, middle and inner ear. Sound is channelled by the **pinna** (outer ear) into the **external auditory canal**, to the eardrum (**tympanic membrane**).

The tympanic membrane marks the commencement of the middle ear. It vibrates with the sound waves, activating the small bones (**ossicles**) behind it. The bone nearest the tympanic membrane is called the **malleus** or **hammer**; this strikes the next bone, appropriately called the **anvil** or **incus**. This transmits the vibrations to the third bone, the **stirrup** or **stapes**, so called because it is stirrup-shaped and also associates with the names of the other bones. The flat side of the stapes connects with a membrane called the **oval window**.

FIGURE 2.9
Diagram of the outer, middle and inner ear

(Not to scale.)

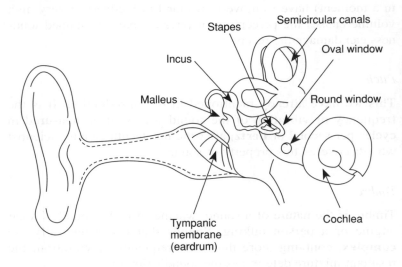

FIGURE 2.10
Diagram of structures in the organ of Corti

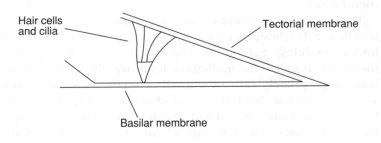

The oval window marks the commencement of the inner ear and covers the aperture in the bone that encases the **cochlea**. This is a complex structure, which resembles a snail shell in appearance (hence its name, from the Greek word for snail). The cochlea is filled with fluid, which can be compressed to allow movement caused by another membrane, called the **round window**.

Inside the cochlea is a receptor called the organ of Corti (**don't ask!**), which consists primarily of three important parts. The **basilar membrane,** which vibrates with the sound waves, in turn vibrates the **hair cells** that are attached to it. The other ends of the hair cells are attached to a rigid, overhead membrane, the **tectoria membrane** (see Figure 2.10). Because this membrane does not move freely, the hair cells and the **cilia** (fine hairs on them) are bent; this produces electrical impulses that are passed along the nerve fibres leaving the cochlea (**cochlear nerve**), to the **auditory nerve**.

Auditory pathways in the brain

Information about auditory stimuli leaving the cochlea, via the cochlear nerve, travels first to the **cochlear nucleus** in the medulla, a subcortical structure of the brain. From here, it passes to the midbrain, then on to the **medial geniculate nucleus** in the thalamus, another subcortical structure. By now, information from each ear is being sent to both sides of the brain; this helps with the **localisation of sound** (see below). Information is now passed to the **primary auditory cortex** for conscious recognition of the sound. Information from each ear is passed to both sides of the cortex. Figure 2.11 shows a diagrammatic representation of the route taken by auditory information from the right ear. As can be seen, it arrives not only at the **ipsilateral** (same side) cortex, but also at the **contralateral** one (opposite side). Information would be transmitted from both ears, and any discrepancy between the arrival times at the cortex and subcortical areas contributes information on where the sound is coming from.

FIGURE 2.11
Central pathways of the auditory system

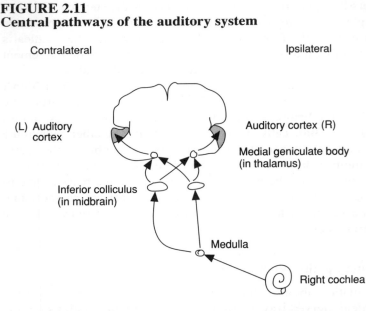

Contralateral   Ipsilateral

(L) Auditory cortex   Auditory cortex (R)

Medial geniculate body (in thalamus)

Inferior colliculus (in midbrain)

Medulla

Right cochlea

Analysis and perception of sound

Detection and perception of pitch

The basilar membrane has differing physical properties along its length and interacts differentially with its surrounding fluids, with the result that high frequencies are mediated nearest the oval window, ranging to low frequencies at the farther end (von Bekesy, 1960). Perception of pitch is liable to damage through physical illness or deterioration due to age; the highest and lowest registers are lost first. The least damage occurs in the middle registers, which is why people with a degree of deafness can hear some sounds and not others; sound perception is not wholly dependent upon loudness.

Detection and perception of loudness

Information regarding the loudness of a stimulus is thought to be dependent on the amount of movement of the hair cells of the cochlea. More intense vibrations produce a more intense force on the cilia, which is encoded by the cochlear nerve as an increased rate of firing. Investigators believe that the loudness of low-frequency sounds is encoded by the number of axons that are active at that time.

Studies using modern equipment have demonstrated that the softest sound that can be detected by the hair cells is that which will move the tip by between 1 and 100 picometres (trillionths of a metre!). No wonder we say we can hear a pin drop! This sensitive mechanism can be damaged by loud noise, especially if it is constant, which is why Health and Safety experts insist on ear protectors for workers in noisy industries. Loudness is measured in decibels (dB); above 85 dB, prolonged exposure leads to nerve deafness. It is possible to become habituated to loud noise, but that does not prevent the physical damage, only the psychological damage. Figure 2.12 outlines some commonly encountered noise levels.

Detection and perception of timbre

Detection of timbre, or complex sounds, is dependent on the auditory system's ability to 'undo' sounds. This detection is due to the ability of the system to recognise which areas of the basilar membrane are being stimulated at any given time.

When you consider that we can listen to an orchestra playing and recognise the independent sounds of several different instruments, the complexity of the analysis being carried out is amazing. Of course, a degree of learning and training is inherent here, but the potential to perform the task is already present.

Localisation of sound

Having two ears, one on each side of the head, is our first aid to locating the source of a sound (**binaural localisation**). There are two main methods of locating sounds: (i) phase differences, and (ii) intensity differences.

Phase differences   Low-pitched sounds may be detected by means of **phase differences**. Sound waves are likely to arrive at each ear at a slightly different phase of their cycles. These minute differences are detected by the basilar membrane and recognised in the auditory neurones in the medulla.

Differences in high-frequency sounds would be difficult to detect by this method because of the small amplitude of high-frequency waves.

Intensity differences   This cue is useful for detecting the source of high-frequency sounds. High-frequency sound waves are absorbed by the head, producing sonic shadowing of any sound that arrives slightly 'off centre' of the two ears. This is why, if a sound is dead centre, it is difficult to say whether it is in front of or behind the head. Information from the organs of Corti, as to which is receiving stimulation first, is recognised in an adjacent area of the medulla.

FIGURE 2.12
Some commonly encountered noise levels

dBa	Noise
140	
130	Pain threshold
120	Pneumatic drill/loud car horn
110	
100	
90	Inside subway train
80	(Permanent damage from long-term noise)
70	Average street-corner traffic
60	Conversational speech
	Typical office noise levels
50	
40	Living room
30	Library
20	Bedroom at night
10	Broadcasting studio
1	Threshold of hearing

Summary

The human auditory system is able to detect and discriminate three main properties of sound: loudness, pitch and timbre. The human ear is a specialised mechanoreceptor. It transforms sound waves into nerve impulses, undoing complex sound input so that we can recognise individual components. We can localise sounds by detecting phase and intensity differences, aided by the fact that both ears are placed on opposite sides of the head.

Self-assessment questions

1. Draw a rough diagram of the middle and inner ear, labelling structures important for the perception of sound.
2. How do humans detect (a) loudness, (b) pitch, and (c) timbre?
3. Describe two ways in which we can localise sound.

SECTION IV   OTHER SENSORY INPUTS

In classical terms, there remain only three more senses to describe: olfaction (smell), taste and touch. However, other important sensory perceptions need to be mentioned, such as the perception of pain, and kinaesthesia, in order to give a more rounded picture of human perceptions.

Olfaction

The sense of smell is a **chemical** sense, recognising chemical molecules of substances that are passing through the olfactory system, which involves areas of the nose and the brain. In vertebrates other than humans, a much larger area of the brain is involved in olfaction, because smell is a much more important cue for many species other than for humans.

Olfactory receptors (see Figure 2.13) are contained within two small areas, each about 2.5 cm square, at the top of the nasal cavity. A sniff draws air upwards to pass these sensitive areas. Aromatic molecules that have dissolved in the air are drawn across the mucous membranes, which contain the receptors, and their chemical components are detected here.

FIGURE 2.13
The olfactory system

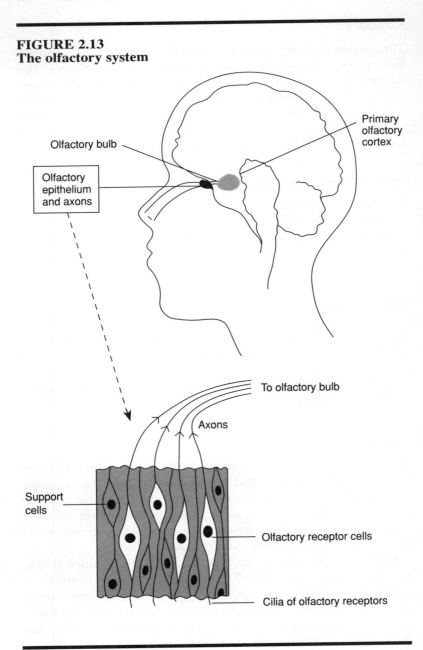

The axons of the olfactory receptors send information to the **olfactory bulbs** at the base of the frontal lobes of the brain. From here, the **olfactory tracts** (nerve pathways) project directly to the **primary olfactory cortex**, as well as sending information to the hypothalamus, which probably integrates information about whether food should be accepted or rejected on the basis of its odour.

Tanabe *et al.* (1974) found that neurones in the olfactory cortex respond selectively to different odours, but as yet scientists have not discovered how we recognise different types of smell. Smell seems to be a highly evocative sense; it can be strongly linked with memories, yet we seem to lack the words to describe it. For example, we would all instantly recognise the smell of freshly baked bread, but can you describe it? It would seem that olfaction is a sense we use for recognition and discrimination, rather than for discussion. The smell of food also helps us decide whether or not it is palatable before we taste it.

Taste

This sense helps us decide which things we eat and which we spit out! Taste, or gustation, is another chemical sense. Molecules of the substance tasted are dissolved in the saliva and stimulate the **taste receptors**. These are situated mainly on the tongue; different regions of the tongue contain different types of receptor, for **sweetness**, **saltiness**, **bitterness** and **sourness** (see Figure 2.14). Generally speaking, sweetness and saltiness are attractive favours, while bitterness and sourness may indicate foods that have 'gone off' and are therefore repugnant.

Taste receptors are quickly worn out; they have an approximate life of ten days before they are replaced. The new cells take over the axonal connections of the degenerated cells. These axons pass via the cranial nerves to the subcortical regions of the medulla and the thalamus. From here information is sent to the **primary gustatory cortex**. Taste is the only sense that projects solely ipsilaterally (i.e. from the left of the tongue to the left side of the brain, and from the right side of the tongue to the right of the brain). Presumably, as we only have one mouth and one tongue, there is no need for crossreferencing as a failsafe system.

FIGURE 2.14
Regions of the tongue involved in taste

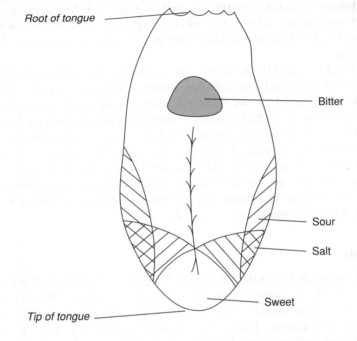

Not only are tastes discriminated at the receptors in the tongue, but responses are also differentiated by different neurones in the cortex (Yamamoto *et al.*, 1981). Complex tastes, involving more than one of the four primary tastes, are analysed at cortical level. The principle common to all the senses holds true here, in that sensation is processed at sensory receptor level, while perception is analysed within the brain.

Somatosenses

These include (a) **cutaneous senses,** such as touch, temperature and pain responses, and (b) **kinaesthesia**, which provides information about body positions and movement.

Cutaneous senses

There are a number of different types of receptor contained in the skin, each with a different job of detection. Skin consists of the **epidermis** (outer layer), **dermis** (a much thicker inner layer) and **subcutaneous tissue**, a deeper layer containing the main nerves, veins and arteries. Cutaneous receptors occur mainly within the dermis. On our bodies, we have **glabrous skin** (hairless), such as on our palms and fingers, and **hairy skin**, as on the rest of the body – although some people are demonstrably more hairy than others!

Pacinian corpuscles   These are the largest sensory end-organs in the body. They are found in the dermis of glabrous skin, the external genitalia, the mammary glands and various internal organs. Each consists of up to 70 layers, wrapped around a single nerve fibre. The corpuscle is filled with viscous fluid. It is sensitive to vibration, and each movement produces a response in the corpuscle's axon.

Ruffini corpuscles   These are found mainly in hairy skin. Smaller than Pacinian corpuscles, they respond to fluttering movements or low-frequency vibration.

Meissner's corpuscles   These are found in papillae, small projections of dermis that have risen upward into the epidermis. These respond to mechanical stimuli, such as touch or pressure.

Merkel's discs   Usually found adjacent to sweat ducts and close to Meissener's corpuscles, they also respond to mechanical stimuli.

Krause end-bulbs   These are found in **mucocutaneous zones**, the junctions between mucous membranes and dry skin, for example the eyelids, edges of lips, penis and clitoris. They consist of loops of axons, forming bulbs, each bulb containing between two and six axons. They respond to mechanical stimuli.

Free nerve endings   Free nerve endings are the simplest type of sensory receptor; they are literally a branching nerve that terminates in the dermis and deeper layers of the epidermis. Some respond to mechanical stimuli, some to warmth or cooling, and some to noxious (unpleasant) stimuli; some respond to two or three of these and are called **polymodal**.

Threshold of sensation

In the bodily areas of high sensitivity, such as the fingers, a single impulse elicited by a stimulus (for example, a momentary touch with the tip of a pencil) is also recognised consciously by the individual. In less sensitive areas, several impulses need to occur before conscious recognition is made. This is why, if a fly alights on the tip of your finger, you are instantly aware of it, but if it alights on your arm or shoulder, you may not be aware until it moves over your skin.

Spatial resolution

Whether a stimulus is coming from a single point or two points on the body is recognised differentially by different body areas, owing to the density of receptors in the skin of that area. Demonstrate this to yourself by the spatial resolution exercise in Box 2.2.

Pain

Considering the trouble it gives us, we still know comparatively little about pain. Free nerve endings appear to respond to painful stimuli, but this is not the only source of information. Intense mechanical stimulation causes a strong reaction in other appropriate receptors, which may be recognised as pain. In addition, most painful stimuli cause tissue damage, which promotes a chemical reaction in the surrounding area, thereby sending chemical messages through the body (Besson *et al.*, 1982). Pain is also the result of tissue damage, for example in burns. Damaged cells release prostaglandin, which sensitises free nerve endings to histamine, another chemical released by damaged cells. (Aspirin blocks the synthesis of prostaglandin, thereby reducing pain.) An investigation into the numerous theories of pain is outside the scope of this small volume.

> ### *BOX 2.2 DEMONSTRATION OF CUTANEOUS SENSATIONS*
>
> 1. Shut your eyes and rub the fingers of one hand over sandpaper and the other on a very smooth surface (polished wood or shiny paper). After 30 seconds change both to a surface of intermediate roughness (say leather or suede). Note the different sensation experienced by both hands.
>
> 2. Place the fingers of one hand into icy cold water and the other hand into hot water (but not hot enough to burn yourself!; this is not a pain experiment!). After 30 seconds put both hands in tepid water. Note the different sensation experienced by both hands.
>
> 3. If you take a pair of dividers and lightly touch a fingertip, two points can be felt at a distance of only 2 mm apart, whereas on the arm you may find a distance of up to 30 mm. Of course, this experiment works best if you can find a friend to act as blindfolded subject while you carry out these investigations!

Kinaesthesia

Even with your eyes closed, or in the dark, you know what position your limbs are in. You can put your finger on the end of your nose with your eyes shut. These feats are due to receptors (primarily Pacinian corpuscles and free nerve endings) in the muscles and where muscles and tendons join, which send information to the brain on muscle stretch, pressure and blood supply. Pacinian corpuscles and free nerve endings are also found in the outer layers of many internal organs. These send information on organic sensations such as pain, pressure and stretch. Kinaesthetic receptors in the muscles of the eye send back information on eye movements and lens accommodation. This helps to determine the movement and location of objects in the visual field.

Ascending pathways and the somatosensory cortex

Axons from somatosensory receptors link into the nerves that ascend the spinal column to subcortical areas of the brain, and thence to the somatosensory cortex. This is an area on each side of the cortex that gives conscious recognition to the information from all the sensory receptors, from all parts of the body.

In the same way that density of receptors in the skin is not equally distributed, there is also differential representation in the cortex for different areas of the body. If the **somatosensory cortex** is not represented as a pie-chart, the head and face get almost half of the pie! The hands then take a quarter, and the remainder of the body shares the other quarter.

SUMMARY

Specialised receptors in the skin provide sensory information on pressure, temperature, vibration and other variable forms of 'touch'. Pain is a complex phenomenon not yet fully understood. Free nerve endings are certainly involved, but we are also aware of pain in other ways. Sensory receptors located where muscles and tendons join send kinaesthetic feedback to give information on the body's movements and position.

SELF-ASSESSMENT QUESTIONS

1. How do we become conscious of smells?
2. What are the processes that enable us to recognise taste?
3. Describe some sensory receptors located in the skin, and their specific purpose.

FURTHER READING

G. von Bekesy, *Experiments in Hearing* (New York: McGraw-Hill, 1960).

N. Carlson, *Physiology of Behaviour* (Boston, Mass.: Allyn & Bacon, 1991).

G. M. Shepherd, *Neurobiology* (Oxford: Oxford University Press, 1988).

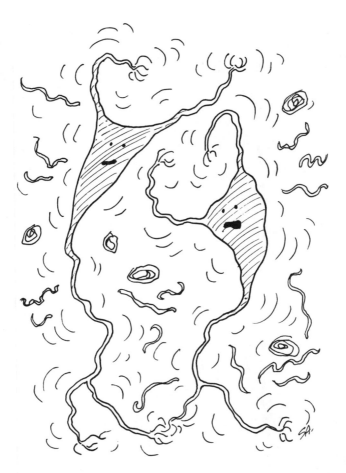

Speaking as a nerve cell, I'd say someone out there's having a ball !

The Nervous System and Behaviour

At the end of this chapter, you should be able to:

- outline the functional divisions of the nervous system;
- describe some of the structures of the central nervous system, and their functions;
- appreciate the role played by neurotransmitters in the nervous system;
- discuss how drugs act on the nervous system; and
- understand the functions of the autonomic nervous system.

INTRODUCTION

The nervous system of the human body is highly complex, more complex than that of any other earthly creature, alive or extinct. This chapter looks at the structure and functions of the nervous system. Structures such as neurones, axons and synapses are described, and their functions outlined. Although the nervous system is a 'whole', it can for ease of examination be theoretically divided according to types of function.

As can be seen from Figure 3.1, the nervous system can be functionally divided in two: the **central nervous system**, which is the centre of human operations, and the **peripheral nervous system**, which, as the name implies, is the remainder, around the 'edges'. These are briefly described below:

FIGURE 3.1
Organisation of the nervous system

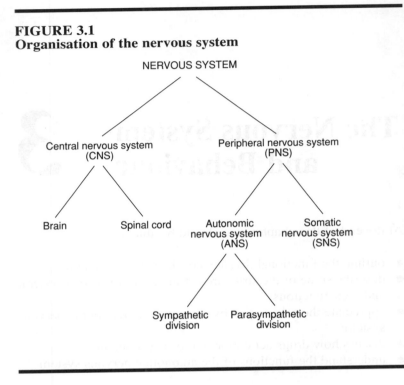

The Central Nervous System

The **central nervous system** (CNS) comprises the **brain** and **spinal cord**. The brain deals with so-called higher functions, integrating messages from the senses, instructing activities, memorising and thinking. The spinal cord carries the major nerve fibres between the brain and other areas such as the limbs and trunk; it also integrates reflex actions. The CNS will be examined in greater detail in Section II of this chapter, as its functions are of particular interest to psychologists.

The Peripheral Nervous System

The **peripheral nervous system** (PNS) includes the **somatic nervous system** (SNS) and the **autonomic nervous system**

(ANS), which both interact with the CNS. The somatic nervous system carries messages to and from the muscles controlling the skeleton, while the autonomic nervous system carries messages to and from the body's internal organs. The ANS is looked at in more detail in Section III of this chapter; it is involved with emotional experiences that are of interest to psychologists studying behaviour.

SECTION I CELL STRUCTURES AND THE COMMUNICATIONS NETWORK

FIGURE 3.2
'See a friend and wave'

Chain of events occurring in the nervous system when you 'see a friend and wave'.

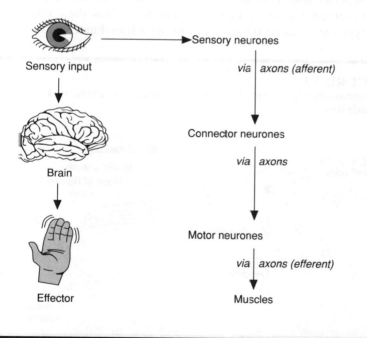

Sensory input	Sensory neurones
	via axons (afferent)
Brain	Connector neurones
	via axons
Effector	Motor neurones
	via axons (efferent)
	Muscles

The major cells in the nervous system are **neurones**. From the electrical activity of a neurone, messages are passed along its **axon** (nerve fibre) towards the next neurone. There are other cells in the nervous system, which provide support for neurones, but these are not described here, as they are of less interest to psychologists.

There are three main types of neurone:

1. **Sensory neurones**, which pick up information from the sensory receptors described in Chapter 2; they send this information onward to the central nervous system (the brain and spinal cord).
2. **Connector neurones**, which are mainly located in the central nervous system, 85 per cent of them being located in the brain. These receive incoming information from the senses or the body's internal environment, 'compute' this information and pass the information on for action to be taken by the individual. This information may be passed to:
3. **Motor neurones**, which send messages from the central nervous system to the muscles and those parts of the body involved in activity. Figure 3.2 illustrates how these three types of neurone function if you see a friend and wave.

FIGURE 3.3
Diagrammatic representation of a neurone, axon and dendrites

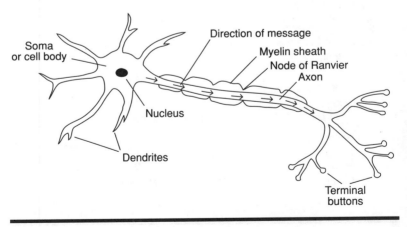

'So how do neurones and axons work?'

Read this explanation in conjunction with consulting Figure 3.3. Information from sensory receptors or from other neurones is picked up by the **receiving dendrites** of a neurone and passed into the **soma**, or **cell body**. If sufficient dendrites receive information, or if the stimulus is sufficiently strong, the cell body will be stimulated to produce an electrical impulse; this is called **firing**. This impulse will pass along the **axon** by an electrochemical process (described in Figure 3.4) until the axon branches out into **sending dendrites** and **terminal buttons**, which transmit to the next neurone. In the case of motor neurones, the axons end in **motor end plates**, which connect directly with the muscle fibres.

The electrochemical process of nervous transmission

Sending nerve impulses around the body is often referred to in terms of **electrical activity**. The actual basis of this electrical activity is a **chemical action**.

All molecules in the body carry either a positive or a negative charge, depending on their particular constituents. For example, potassium (K^+) and sodium (Na^+) are both positive, whereas chlorine (Cl^-) is negative.

Inside the axons (nerve fibres), there are primarily potassium (K^+) ions and large, negatively charged protein molecules. Outside the axon are sodium (Na^+) and chloride (Cl^-) ions. The wall of the axon is normally impermeable (permits no entry or exit) to moleules, and an active transport system, called the **sodium pump**, transports Na^+ molecules to the outside of the membrane. This is in order to maintain the **resting potential** of the axon as negative compared with the outside environment.

When a neurone is stimulated by neurotransmitters to 'fire' an impulse along its axon, this resting potential is disturbed and chemical changes take place. The membrane is **depolarised** and positively charged Na^+ ions rush in from outside. These are quickly retransported by the sodium pump. During this change of electrical activity, an **action potential** occurs (see Figure 3.4(a)). This represents the electrical activity in that section of the axon. In reconstituting this section of the membrane, the next section of

membrane is depolarised, and the chemical and electrical activity
is repeated over again.

FIGURE 3.4
The electrochemical process of nervous transmission

(a) Action potential caused by changes of polarity in the axon

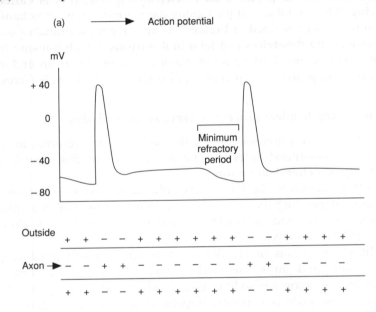

(b) The pattern of firing produced by stimulation of an axon

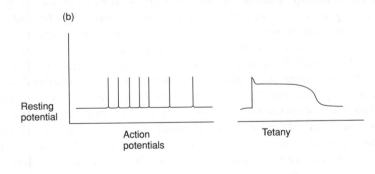

In this way, firing proceeds along the axon, producing a series of action potentials (often called **spikes**, for obvious reasons!). The spikes are always the same size, although the spacing between them may vary, according to the rate or intensity of neuroneal activity.

The constant size of the action potential is due to what is called the **all-or-none-law**. An neurone never half-fires; it either fires or it does not, thereby producing a consistent size action potential. If the neuroneal stimulation is weak, impulses will not be passed along the axon. Firing will not occur until sufficient stimulation is present to be above the **threshold of response**, the level at which depolarisation will occur. If weak impulses have to be summated (added together) before firing can occur, this will be shown as a slow resonse rate of firing (wide spaces between the spikes). After each spike comes a period (milliseconds only) during which the axon cannot fire again (the **absolute refractory period**), when the sodium ions are transported out and the membrane reconstitutes. However, if the stimulation is abnormally intense, firing may be maintained without any refractory period. This is called **tetany** (see Figure 3.4(b)). This is what happens to the nervous system if the tetanus virus is introduced into the body.

Information can only be transmitted one way along an axon: there is no two-way traffic, which would cause chaos!

All but the smallest axons in the human body are covered by a **myelin sheath**, which is punctuated at intervals by the **nodes of Ranvier**. Any decrease in the elecrochemical activity in the axon is regenerated at the next node of Ranvier, which provides a burst of activity to send the message onward. This is why the axon's conduction process is called **saltatory conduction** (from the Latin *saltare*, to dance): it proceeds in leaps and bounds!

The synapse

The area where an axon connects with the dendrite of another neurone is called the **synapse** (see Figure 3.5). Axons do not join directly onto the dendrites or the cell body of the next neurone; there is a gap, called the **synaptic cleft**. The electrical activity of the axon cannot proceed across the synaptic cleft, so a different process bridges the gap.

Chemicals called **transmitter substances** are contained in the terminal buttons of the sending dendrites. When these are electrically stimulated by the axon, they are released across the synaptic cleft, onto specialised **receptor sites** in the receiving dendrites of the next neurone in the chain.

FIGURE 3.5
The synapse

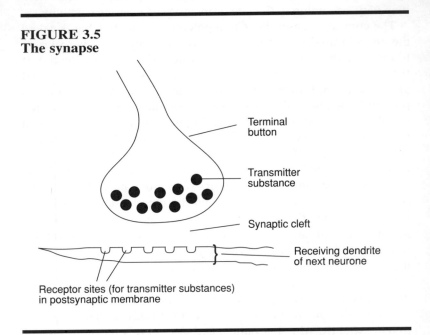

If sufficient transmitters are received by sufficient dendrites, this will prompt the next neurone to fire, and the message is passed on. If insufficient transmitter is received, the message will lapse. This system also prevents random firings (generated by the brain itself, which hates inactivity) from being passed on as genuine messages.

In addition, certain transmitters have an **inhibitory** action, that is to say they discourage firing. A balance of activating and inhibitory transmitters ensures the passage of genuine messages. However **psychoactive drugs**, such as amphetamines (see Section IV), often mimic the action of certain neurotransmitters, which is why people under the influence of drugs 'see' and 'hear' things that are not really there.

Once the transmitters have caused the neurone to fire, they have completed their task and need to be deactivated, or they will continue to instruct firing. They are deactivated by **reuptake**, or reabsorption into the membrane of the dendrites from which they came. A few, notably **acetylcholine** (a neurotransmitter active in, for example, the 'memory' areas of the brain) are deactivated by **enzymes**, which lock on, rendering them inactive, and break them down to their constituent chemicals for recirculation and later reassembly. Acetylcholinesterase, the enzyme which deactivates acetylcholine, is extremely energetic: one molecule can deactivate 5000 molecules of transmitter!

NEURAL NETWORKS

Of course, neurones do not work in isolation or even simply in long 'strings', as Figure 3.3 may have implied. There are millions of interconnections between neurones, and this facilitates the flow of information to other areas. Are these simply random connections or is there some meaningful pattern?

Cell assemblies

As early as 1950, Donald Hebb suggested that learning is consolidated in the brain by activation of **cell assemblies**, groups of neurones that fire systematically to respond to a specific stimulus. This causes structural changes to the cells, possibly even the growth of new synapses. As this reoccurs, the cell assembly 'learns' and responds each time, forming the neural basis of memory.

This idea is similar to a recent approach to modelling the function of neural circuits, called **neural networks**. **Connectionist models** (see Figure 3.6) are computer models that simulate the activity of neurones; connections may be either excitatory or inhibitory. Neural networks can be taught to recognise a particular stimulus, and connections can be strengthened by reinforcement, or an inhibitory system can be inbuilt to refine responses to one particular stimulus. A network can be 'shown' a particular stimulus and its output monitored. After several presentations of the same stimulus, the output shows a strong and reliable response pattern.

FIGURE 3.6
A simple neural network model

Connectionist models of the brain suggest a neural network of connections (depicted by arrows) linking neurones that are involved in joint activities, such as responding to a specific stimulus.

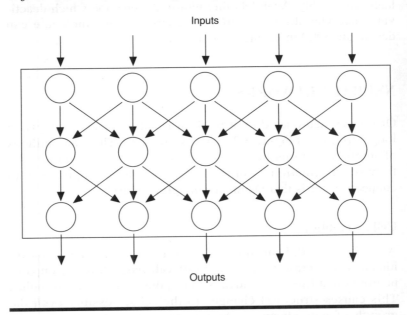

1. *Generalisation.* When a network has learned to recognise a specific stimulus and is then shown a similar stimulus, its output pattern will resemble the one it gives to the known stimulus.
2. *Discrimination.* If a network learns several similar stimuli, it will learn to distinguish between them and produce different output patterns for each.
3. *Degradation.* If a network or its connections (synapses) are damaged, the network does not cease functioning but produces a deterioration of performance, usually relevant to the level of damage.

As more is learned about neural networks, more realistic models are being constructed. The brain almost certainly contains many thousands of networks, each involved with individual functions and exchanging information with other networks. How closely network models represent the activity of the brain is a question still being refined. Connectionist scientists are constantly refining techniques modelling neural networks. These are areas of research that show the greatest promise of explaining, in the not-too-distant future, how the human central nervous system works. For example, the following simulation experiment used present-generation supercomputers to identify photographs of outdoor scenes. A neural network was 'trained' to classify regions in terms of segmented images from an image database. Eleven classifications were set up, including trees, houses, pavement, sky, road and car.

On presentation of the test photographs of outdoor scenes, between 70 and 81 per cent of images and areas of the photographs were correctly identified by the computer. This demonstrated that features can be extracted in parallel and labelled in parallel (Campbell *et al.*, 1995).

Summary

The basic unit of the nervous system is a neurone, which sends impulses along axons, through terminal buttons at the synapse, to the dendrites of other axons. Messages are conveyed along axons by an electrochemical process. The rate of firing conveys further information. Sensory neurones convey information to and from the senses, motor neurones to and from the skeletal system. Connector neurones are located mainly in the brain, with some in the spinal cord. Connectionist models attempt to explain how the neurones in the brain are interconnected in activity-related groups, which may represent human learning patterns.

Self-assessment questions

1. What are the similarities and differences between sensory, connector and motor neurones?
2. Draw a diagram of a synapse and explain briefly how it 'works'.

3. Reread the section The electrochemical process of nervous transmission. Now explain briefly, in your own words, how transmission of impulses takes place.
4. What is the all-or-none law?
5. What are connectionist models?

SECTION II   THE CENTRAL NERVOUS SYSTEM

The CNS is the centre of neural activity; integrating incoming information, organising thought processes, making decisions and issuing instructions to the body. It comprises the brain and spinal cord; these are described below. Damage to the CNS is not regenerated (repaired), as occurs with other areas of the body.

THE BRAIN

The brain is soft and floats in its own waterbed for protection. It cannot feel pain if damaged directly, as it has no pain receptors. An adult brain weighs about 1.361 kg and contains around 100 billion neurones, which die in vast numbers and are not regenerated. The brain receives about one-fifth of the blood pumped out by the heart; it needs the glucose and oxygen in the blood in order to function efficiently. If deprived of oxygen for more than three or four minutes, irreparable damage is likely to occur.

Structure of the brain

The brain is divided into two halves, called **hemispheres**. The outer covering of the brain is called the **neocortex** ('neo' meaning 'new', as this only occurs in animals that have evolved comparatively recently; 'neocortex' is usually simply abreviated to **cortex**). Owing to the quantity of neurones in the cortex, it appears grey in colour, giving rise to the common reference to 'grey matter'. Other structures contained within the brain are referred to as **subcortical structures**, often called 'white matter'.

The **blood–brain barrier** is a filter system that prevents some substances from reaching the brain even when carried in the bloodstream. This barrier works both ways, and some substances produced by the brain do not enter the body and would be regarded by the body as 'foreign'. Some investigators believe that multiple sclerosis is due to virus damage of the blood–brain barrier, which then permits CNS myelin protein to enter the bloodstream and be transported round the body. This mobilises the immune system against the 'foreign invader', which then destroys the myelination in the CNS. With its insulation gone, axons cannot keep their messages separate and they become scrambled, so activities cannot be instructed clearly.

Areas of the brain

The cortex

This is only approximately 4 mm thick, and covers the entire surface of the brain. Its many convolutions and folds means that a greater surface area is contained within the small space inside the skull. In fact, if you unfolded and ironed out the cortex, it would cover approximately 0.232m².

The four lobes of the cortex   For ease of reference, each hemisphere is divided into four lobes: **frontal**, **parietal**, **occipital** and **temporal** (named after the bones of the skull that cover them, see Figure 3.7). For decades now, physiologists and psychologists have been 'mapping' areas of the cortex according to their functions.

Conscious processes such as thinking and decision making are thought to be controlled by the frontal lobes of the cortex. It is also thought that memories are stored by the cortex, but the exact method of storage has not yet been determined.

Motor and somatosensory areas   Some areas are delineated in Figure 3.7, such as the visual and auditory cortex, as discussed in Chapter 2. Along the **central sulcus** (or fold) is the **primary motor cortex** and its associated area next to it, which contain neurones involved in movement. The other side of the central sulcus is the **somatosensory cortex**, which integrates information from the body senses, such as touch, pressure and pain.

This mapping of areas of the cortex seems directly opposed to Lashley's **law of mass action**, which suggested that the cortex functioned as a whole rather than as discrete areas. However, Lashley was looking at the cortex with the intention of identifying where learning and memory occurred. These functions, as mentioned previously, do not seem to be specifically located in one area of the cortex but are spread throughout it.

FIGURE 3.7
Some areas of the cerebral cortex

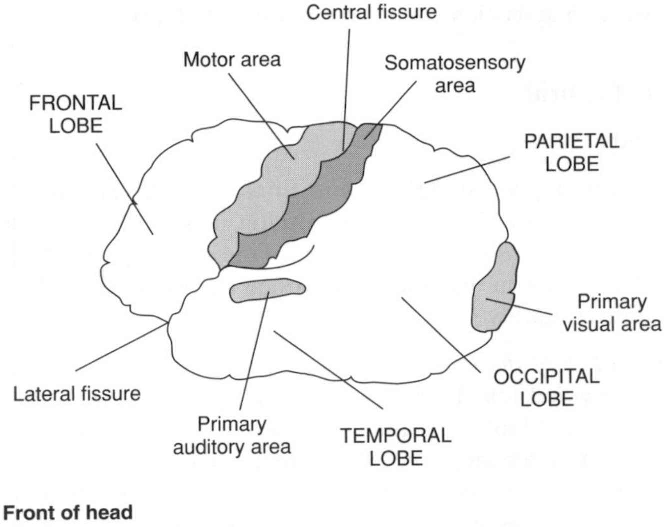

Front of head

Functions of the two hemispheres   The cortex of the two hemispheres may appear identical to look at, but in humans one hemisphere is usually **dominant**. In most people, this is the left hemisphere, which controls the right side of the body. Some functions are only contained in one hemisphere, for example speech, which is usually in the left hemisphere. In some left-handed people, speech is on the right, where the two hemispheres have been 'switched'; in other cases, left-handedness may have occurred for other reasons (Beaumont, 1988).

The non-dominant hemisphere, usually the right, appears to be responsible for functions such as spatial localisation (being aware of the relationships of objects in the spatial field). This may be of use to humans in many ways, for example, for architects, artists and tennis and squash players. It is interesting to note how many top-class tennis players and artists are also left-handed. These people presumably have their spatial representation in their dominant hemisphere; does this therefore mean that their speech centres are located in their non-dominant hemisphere? If so, with what effect? Further studies would be necessary to answer these questions in relation to specific individuals.

Box 3.1   *LOCALISATION OF SPEECH (AN EXAMPLE OF LATERALISATION)*

Language areas of the brain

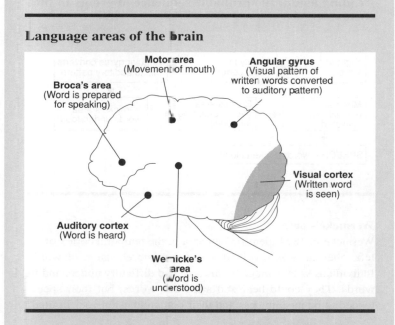

In most people, speech is localised in the left hemisphere of the cortex. Investigation has identified several specific areas associated with the comprehension and production of speech.

Broca's area
During the nineteenth century, Broca was investigating speech loss in a patient and identified an area of damage to the cerebral cortex, in the left frontal lobe. Similar damage to the right frontal lobe did not usually produce loss of speech. It appeared that in

this area, words were formulated or prepared for speech. (The actual production of speech also involves the motor cortex, which controls the tongue, mouth and larynx.)

Incomplete damage to Broca's area means that individuals have difficulty formulating words. Nouns are often produced in the singular, and less important words are often omitted. There is no difficulty understanding spoken or written language, which suggests to investigators that areas other than this are responsible for the comprehension of speech.

Reading aloud: the probable sequence of events in the cortex

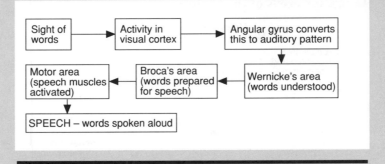

Wernicke's area

Wernicke in 1874 identified an area in the temporal cortex of the left lobe that was involved with the comprehension of words. Individuals with damage to this area had difficulty understanding words. They could hear and articulate words, but their speech tended to be meaningless and their comprehension very limited.

Angular gyrus

This is an area of the brain involved in reading. It matches a written word to its auditory code. The flow diagram above shows a representation of all the areas of the brain involved in the process of reading aloud. It is no wonder that so many people have difficulty with this, apart from the embarrassment of being 'on stage'.

Scientists are still not sure whether functions other than speech are localised in a specific hemisphere; it is not permissible to carry out true experiments on people's brains, purely out of scientific interest, as we discussed in Chapter 1. Instead, psychologists often take the opportunity to examine the functioning of patients who have had brain surgery. This was the basis for Sperry's work; his patients had received brain surgery to prevent the spread of epileptic seizures that were becoming life-threatening. Once recovered from the operation, his patients were asked to carry out a variety of perceptual tasks, the results of which give us some insight into the functioning of the two hemispheres (see Box 3.2).

BOX 3.2   IN TWO MINDS?

Sperry (1968) reported the behavioural, cognitive and perceptual outcomes of **commisurotomy**, the so-called 'split brain' operation. This is an operation that severs the corpus callosum and the fibres that connect the two hemispheres across this structure. The operation is performed rarely, in specifically identified patients with severe epilepsy, to prevent the electrical disturbances spreading from one hemisphere to the other.

Careful investigations prior to the operation assured Sperry that patients' brain functioning would not be significantly impaired, but there would be postoperative differences. These were to be the subject of his further studies.

After the operations, all patients were either seizure-free or experienced only minor seizures. None appeared to have changes of personality or loss of intelligence. Perceptual responses were, however, affected; Sperry suggested that the two hemispheres appeared to be functioning independently, almost as two separate brains'.

For example:

1. If a visual stimulus was presented to a patient's right visual field (by use of a central screen), and an appropriate response made, when the same stimulus was then presented to the left visual field, the patient responded as though it had not been seen before.

2. In reading and writing (bearing in mind that in most right-handed people the left hemisphere mediates speech and reading responses): if visual material was presented to the right visual field, it could be described in speech and writing in the normal way, being mediated by the left visual hemisphere. However, if an object was presented to the left visual field, patients were unable to name it, but could select a similar object from a choice of objects available. In both cases, information appeared not to be passed from one hemisphere to the other; each hemisphere was 'doing what it does best', but independently.

The right side of the brain is capable of recognising and producing some language, but this is limited, although some people have language represented bilaterally (Beaumont, 1988). Ornstein (1986) suggests that the left hemisphere is specialised for analytical verbal and mathematical functions, processing information sequentially (one item at a time, in straight lines), while the right hemisphere is impressionistic, holistic and processes several items at the same time. Sperry's work would seem to substantiate claims for lateralisation of functions (different functions being mediated by separate hemispheres), although some are undoubtedly represented bilaterally.

Cohen (1975) suggests that it may be invalid to generalise from these patients, who have experienced abnormal brain functioning for some time, to normal people. She suggests that the hemispheres normally function together, using a mixture of 'left' and 'right' skills. Mackay (1987) investigated whether split-brain patients demonstrated two separate forms of consciousness or free will, but decided that there was insufficient evidence to assume this, although they occasionally appeared to be unaware of decisions made by one hemisphere or the other.

Subcortical structures

Figure 3.8 shows some of the subcortical structures of the brain; the functions of some of these are described briefly below, and these structures will be mentioned again during the course of this book. The pituitary gland is described in Chapter 4, as it is part of the endocrine system, but is included in this diagram in order to demonstrate its whereabouts.

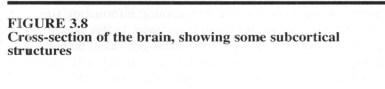

FIGURE 3.8
Cross-section of the brain, showing some subcortical structures

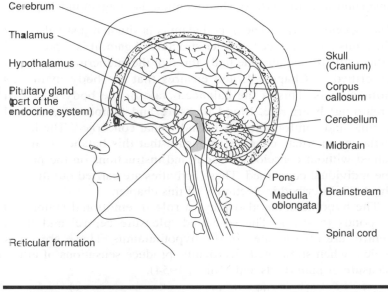

The brainstem   Structurally, this is an extension of the spinal cord and contains structures such as the **pons**, the **medulla oblongata** and the **reticular activating system** or **reticular formation**. Parts of the brainstem control our most basic and vital functions, such as breathing, waking, sleeping and maintaining our heartbeat.

The reticular formation   This structure consists of clusters of neurones situated at the top of the brainstem. It is important in arousal and wakefulness. If the reticular formation is extensively damaged, it may not be possible to arouse a patient.

The thalamus   The thalamus consists of an egg-shaped cluster of neurones situated just above the brainstem. There is a thalamus in each hemisphere, both acting in unison. Most subcortical structures are represented **bilaterally** (in both hemispheres). Some of the neurones in the thalamus receive incoming information from the senses and direct it onward through the brain. In this way, they act as a relay station; for example, the lateral geniculate bodies of the visual system (mentioned in Chapter 2) are situated in the thalamus.

Other thalamic neurones play an important part in the control of sleep and wakefulness; we shall mention these again in Chapter 7.

The hypothalamus   The hypothalamus is situated just below the thalamus and is a much smaller structure. Again, it is represented bilaterally. It regulates the body through the endocrine system, as described in Chapter 4, and ensures that the body maintains **homeostasis**. This is the balanced state of the body in which breathing, heart rate, blood pressure and temperature are all normal and comfortable for the individual concerned. The hypo-thalamus instructs changes to ensure that this balance is main-tained without conscious thought and instructions on the part of the individual concerned. These activities are carried out through the ANS described in Section V of this chapter.

The hypothalamus also plays a role in emotional states and responds to stress. The so-called 'pleasure centre' and 'pain centre' are also located in the hypothalamus. These are areas which, when stimulated electrically, produce sensations of either pleasure or pain (Olds and Milner, 1954).

The limbic system   The limbic system is a group of brain struc-tures sometimes called the 'old brain' because they are present in animals further down the phylogenetic scale. The limbic system has close links with the hypothalamus and appears to impose extra control over some of the instinctive and emotional responses mediated by the hypothalamus, by inhibiting them.

Another area of the limbic system, the **hippocampus**, is involved with the laying down of new memories. If the hippocampus is damaged by a virus infection or surgically removed, the patient will not remember new people met after that time nor fresh events (anterograde amnesia). Old, long-standing memories and old friends will be recalled with no problem, however, as these are already 'set' (Squire, 1986). It is possible that emotions are important in selecting what we must learn; great fear will teach us never to cross the motorway on foot again!

The **amygdala** is another area in the limbic system. It is also involved with the control of emotional responses. Lesions in the amygdala often result in undirected aggressive responses, as though the emotional response cannot be co-ordinated properly.

Corpus callosum This is a physical rather than a functional structure. It is the bridge where nerve fibres cross over from left to right, and vice versa. If this structure is severed (as in commisurotomy), information is no longer passed to the other side of the brain, with some strange behavioural results (See Box 3.2, above).

The cerebellum Situated at the back of the brain, this structure is associated with co-ordinating movement to make it smooth rather than jerky. It also stores memory of movement patterns, so that you do not have to concentrate on how to walk or run, and ensures that once you have learned to ride a bike, you will never forget!

Although each brain area may have its own specific role, activities are interrelated and therefore areas of the brain must be interrelated. Damage to one area of the brain may well affect the functioning of other areas. Once damaged, the brain, unlike other areas of the body, does not regenerate. There are claims from individuals that they regain functions, but this is unusual except in the case of young children, in whom **plasticity** occurs. This is the ability of the young brain to take over the roles of damaged areas, presumably because functions are still being delineated (Rose, 1976).

THE SPINAL CORD

Running the length of the body, from brain to 'tail', the spinal cord is housed within the vertebrae of the spinal column. It consists of collections of axons running to or from the brain to various parts of the body. Pairs of major nerves emerge at specific points along the spine, to enervate the arms, the legs and areas of the trunk.

The spinal cord does not always send information to the brain and wait for a reply; it has its own quick system for simple tasks, known as the **reflex arc** (see Figure 3.9). If you step on something sharp when barefoot, the information travels via the sensory input to a sensory neurone, and then to connector neurones housed in the spinal column. These immediately instruct the motor neurones of the leg to contract, pulling the leg away from the point of contact.

Simple reflexes may only involve sensory and motor neurones, for example, where the bent knee is tapped and jerks upwards. This is the kind of test you may have seen carried out by doctors to see whether the reflex arc is functioning effectively.

FIGURE 3.9
A three-neurone reflex arc

Sensations pass via the sensory neurone to the connector neurone, which instructs the motor neurone to contract the muscle, thereby withdrawing from the 'sharp' stimulus.

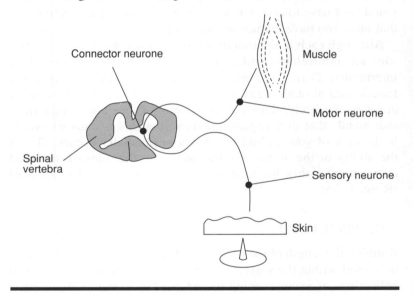

Summary

The brain is the organ that controls the human organism. It integrates and makes sense of input, makes decisions, remembers what is important and instructs the body to carry out response behaviours. The spinal cord carries the major nerve fibres between the body and the brain, and can implement reflex activity without conscious intervention.

Together, the brain and spinal cord constitute the CNS. If damaged, it does not regenerate. Neurones that die are not replaced, but we start out with so many that we never run out of them!

Self-assesment questions

1. Trace or copy Figures 3.7 and 3.8, including the arrows but not the labels. Now close the book and fill in the labels on your diagrams. Check your answers and correct if necessary.
2. Briefly describe the functions of three subcortical areas.
3. What is 'plasticity'?
4. What happens during a reflex action?
5. Describe the problems that may be experienced after a 'split-brain' operation.

SECTION III   NEUROCHEMICALS

Among the chemicals circulating in the brain are some which have direct bearing on the behaviour of the individual. These include **neurotransmitters,** which we have mentioned and will now examine in more detail, together with **neuromodulators.** In addition, **pheromones** are briefly described here, while **hormones** are discussed fully in Chapter 4. Finally, we will look at the way in which psychoactive drugs act on the brain, in the light of our understanding of brain chemicals. It is outside the scope of this book to examine the processes of addiction, although this will be mentioned from time to time.

NEUROTRANSMITTERS

Neurotransmitters are the chemicals released at the synapse. They are involved in the transmission of messages, as previously described. Their action can be either **excitatory** (promoting action) or **inhibitory** (lessening activity), depending on the site where they are acting. To date, at least 40 neurotransmitters have been identified, but we will confine ourselves to discussing only a few, those identified as being of prime importance and of greatest interest to psychologists.

Acetylcholine

This is the transmitter substance that is found in the hippo-campus, as we mentioned earlier, and surrounding areas of the brain. This location suggests that it is involved with memory and learning. The same transmitter is also found at the neuro-muscular junction (that is, where axons from motor neurones connect with muscles) and is involved with movement of the skeletal system.

The main difference between these two systems lies in the receptor sites: the skeletal receptors are **nicotinic receptors**, because they are stimulated by nicotine, a poison found in tobacco leaves, whereas the receptors in the CNS are primarily **muscarinic receptors**, stimulated by muscarine, a poison found in mushrooms. These different receptors, while both detecting acetylcholine, are linked to different physiological systems, which then respond differentially.

The monoamines

These are a chemically similar group of neurotransmitters, all of which have specific actions, so will be described individually. Three (dopamine, norepinephrine and epinephrine) form a related subgroup, called the **catecholamines**, dopamine being the precursor (or previous chemical step) of the other two.

Dopamine

Dopamine has been identified as a transmitter involved in move-ment, especially the initiation of movements, attention and learning. It is synthesised in the CNS in the neurones of the **substantia nigra** (see Figure 3.10) and circulates through the **dopamine circuit**.

Degeneration of these neurones can occur with age, meaning that not enough dopamine is produced; this causes **Parkinson's**

d:sease. This is characterised by delay in initiating movement, a shuffling walk, tremors of the limbs while inactive and an inability to regain balance. Treatment to date involves the administration of L-dopa, a synthetic form of the precursor of dopamine, which alleviates the distressing symptoms, at least for a while.

FIGURE 3.10
The influence of dopamine pathways on movement

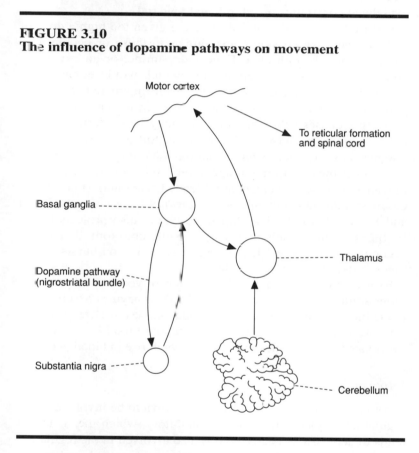

Recent research has suggested that a cause of some cases of Parkinson's disease may be the chemical MPTP, which attacks the dopaminergic neurones. Several years ago, a number of young people took illicit drugs that contained MPTP. This had the effect of destroying their dopaminergic neurones, effectively making them premature sufferers of Parkinson's disease (Langston *et al.*, 1983). Currently, new operations are being pioneered, involving brain surgery, to alleviate Parkinsonian symptoms. The transplant of dopaminergic neurones from a human foetus is not being carried out in Great Britain, owing to the ethical constraints of using foetal material.

If sufferers of Parkinson's disease are given too high a dose of L-dopa, they exhibit symptoms similar to those of people who suffer from schizophrenia. Excess dopamine, or an excessive number of dopamine receptor sites, which would enhance the action of circulating dopamine, has been implicated in schizophrenia. It would be too simplistic, however, to state that excess dopamine causes schizophrenia; this may be the effect, rather than the primary cause of the problem. Sufferers from schizophrenia may experience hallucinations (auditory and/or visual), and sometimes exhibit strange motor movements, excessive movements or no movement at all (called catatonia). (For a fuller description of schizophrenia, see *Individual Differences*, by Birch and Hayward, 1994.) The dopamine circuit also projects to the limbic system, which is involved with emotion; this could account for the mood changes and aggressive outbursts sometimes suffered by schizophrenics.

Excess dopamine in the CNS is destroyed by the enzyme **monoamine oxidase** (MAO for short!). This enzyme also circulates in the blood, where it deactivates certain amines that are present in some foods, such as cheese, chocolate and broad beans. Unless deactivated, these amines could cause a high rise in blood pressure.

Serotonin

Serotonin (also called 5HT) has been shown to be involved in the regulation of mood. Its action is inhibitory, which means that it tends to depress CNS activity. It is also involved in the regulation of pain, in the control of eating, sleeping and arousal, and also in the control of dreaming. At most synapses, its effects are inhibitory rather than excitatory, and its behavioural effects are largely inhibitory.

Serotonin is present in the midbrain, in a cluster of cells called the **raphe nuclei**, and in the **medulla**. These structures send nerve fibres to the forebrain, the cerebellum and the spinal cord, which suggests a widespread method of influencing arousal, sensory perception, emotion and thought processes.

Norepinephrine

Norepinephrine is chemically exactly the same as noradrenaline, and epinephrine is identical to adrenaline. Many books interchange these terms, but I have decided to use the terms 'norepinephrine' and 'epinephrine' for the neurotransmitters and 'adrenaline' and 'noradrenaline' when referring to the hormones. All are produced by the core of the adrenal glands (see Chapter 4).

Noradrenergic neurones in the brain are situated in the lower brainstem and are mainly involved in arousal and wakefulness. In the CNS, norepinephrine plays an excitatory role and is more widespread than epinephrine, which has an inhibitory effect. Both transmitters are present in the axons of the autonomic nervous system, which is described in Section V. Noradrenergic axons release their neurotransmitter through swellings on the axon (called **varicosities**, see Figure 3.11), rather than from terminal buttons, as do other neurotransmitters.

Like dopamine, excess norepinephrine and epinephrine are destroyed by the enzyme MAO.

FIGURE 3.11
Norepinephrine is released from *varicosities* (swellings) in the axons, rather than from terminal buttons

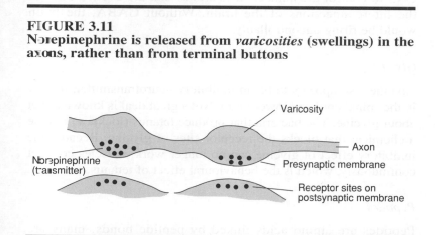

Varicosity

Axon

Norepinephrine
(transmitter)

Presynaptic membrane

Receptor sites on
postsynaptic membrane

Amino acid transmitters

This group of transmitters differs from the others as amino acids are used for protein synthesis by all cells in the brain. However, three of them play a particularly important role as neurotransmitters; these are (i) glutamic acid, (ii) GABA (gamma-aminobutyric acid), and (iii) glycine.

Glutamic acid

Often called **glutamate**, glutamic acid is found throughout the brain and appears to be the principal excitatory neurotransmitter. It is produced liberally by the cells' metabolic processes. Monosodium glutamate, found in a number of manufactured foods, also contains glutamic acid, and people who are hypersensitive to glutamate may experience neurological symptoms, such as dizziness, or hyperactivity, when they eat foods containing too much glutamate.

GABA

GABA is produced from glutamic acid (its precursor) by the action of an enzyme that modifies its chemical structure. GABA has a widespread distribution throughout the brain and spinal cord, and exerts an inhibitory influence. This is essential in the CNS to control the number of neurones that are excited through the interconnections of the brain. Without GABA, the brain would be firing uncontrollably.

Glycine

Glycine also appears to be an inhibitory neurotransmitter, mainly in the spinal cord and lower brain. Not a great deal is known as yet about glycine. The bacteria that produce tetanus (lockjaw) release a chemical that blocks the receptor sites of glycine. Because the inhibitory effect of glycine can no longer work, muscles contract continuously, which is the behavioural effect of tetanus.

Peptides

Peptides are amino acids linked by peptide bonds; many are released by neurones. Some serve as neurotransmitters, others appear to act as neuromodulators. Psychologists are particularly interested in the opiate-like peptides classed as endorphins, because of the effect they have on behaviour.

Endorphins and enkephalins

Endorphins. Early work by Pert *et al.* (1974) identified opiate receptors in the brain and endorphin-containing neurones in the hypothalamus. Projections reach the amygdala and the higher brainstem. Endorphins act as pain-reducing agents – the brain's own anaesthetic.

Enkephalins. These are chemically similar to endorphins but occupy different areas of the brain. Identified by Hughes *et al.* (1975), enkephalins are widespread throughout the nervous system and, like endorphins, appear to have the function of pain modulation. In the peripheral nervous system, enkephalins are found in the adrenal medulla (in the endocrine system, see Chapter 4) and in the nerve fibres of the intestinal system.

Functionally, it has been suggested that it is the endorphins and enkephalins that are mobilised during activity such as fighting. They will then modify any pain suffered until the fight is over and the individual can retire to care for the wounds sustained.

The enkephalins have been suggested as being instrumental in many previously unexplained phenomena, such as acupuncture. It is suggested the needles may be stimulating the localised production of enkephalins. The production of endorphins and enkephalins may also help to explain why a rugby player might complete the game and find afterwards that he has a broken collar bone. Perhaps it may explain a phenomenon you yourself may have observed. For the past few hundred years at least, vets and blacksmiths have been applying a twitch to horses who are difficult to handle. (A twitch is a piece of rope, wound around the horse's upper lip, and tightened.) It sounds cruel, and many people have thought that the pain of the lip was taking all the horse's attention and letting the vet get on with job in hand. But if you watch a horse with a twitch, the eyes droop and the animal appears calm, almost sleepy, not at all like an animal in pain. Perhaps this area stimulates the production of enkephalins, which induces a calming effect. Perhaps we humans are not so different either. Next time you feel very upset, try pinching your top lip between thumb and finger for a while – does it work for you?

NEUROMODULATORS

Neuromodulators are chemicals that are diffused widely throughout the brain, only not occuring at the synapse, as do neuro-transmitters, or within specific pathways. They act in conjunction with neurotransmitters, as their name implies, modulating the activity of surrounding chemicals. Some receptor sites are organised to receive both neurotransmitters and neuromodulators.

PHEROMONES

Pheromones are chemicals that are released by the body through sweat, urine or the excretions of specialised glands. These chemicals are detected by the recipient's sense of smell. In animals other than humans, they are primary signals for attracting mates and initiating sexual behaviour, by acting upon the hormonal systems of potential mates. In addition, these chemicals are used as 'markers' for delineating territories and repelling would-be adversaries.

Humans produce pheromones, and recent research has attempted to identify how important these are in their original attraction/repellant roles. As proportionally less of the human brain is used for identifying and integrating smell-patterns (we do not go sniffing at each other for identification, as dogs and cats do!), it is probable that these chemicals are less important to us than to animals farther down the phylogenetic scale.

Summary

Neurotransmitters act at the synapse and are the CNS 'failsafe' system, to ensure that only genuine messages are passed onwards. Not all neurotransmitters are diffused throughout the brain, but each of them is usually specific to an area or circuit. Mood is influenced by the activity of specfic neurotransmitters, through the areas of the brain where they are generated, to the areas of the brain to which they send projections.

Neuromodulators are chemicals that circulate more widely through the nervous system, moderating the activity of neuro-transmitters, usually through adjacent receptor sites. Pheromones are chemicals that are exuded by the body to give out signals. In humans, these may convey information about the sex and identity of the individual, but do not seem to have such an important role as in other animals.

Self-assessment questions

1. What are neurotransmitters?
2. Write a paragraph on each of the following: (a) acetylcholine, (b) dopamine, (c) norepinephrine, (d) serotonin, (e) endorphins/enkephalins and (f) GABA.
3. Briefly describe: (a) neuromodulators, and (b) pheromones.

SECTION IV HOW SOME PSYCHOACTIVE DRUGS ACT ON THE CNS

There are five broad categories of psychoactive drug used for medical purposes: (i) minor tranquillisers, (ii) neuroleptics, (iii) stimulants, (iv) antidepressants, and (v) opiates, for the control of strong pain. Other nonmedical psychoactive drugs will also be mentioned. Many psychoactive drugs are addictive, producing physiological or psychological dependence, and are usually administered for short periods of time only.

Minor tranquillisers

One class of these drugs is the benzodiazepines, which appear to reduce anxiety, promote sleep and produce muscle relaxation by stimulating the **GABA receptors**. As the effect of GABA is inhibitory, as we discussed above, the resultant neural inhibition reduces the anxiety effects. Three commonly prescribed drugs are Valium (diazepam), Librium (chlordiazepoxide) and Mogadon (nitrazepam); all are addictive if continued for long periods. Diazepam is also prescribed for the quick cessation of epileptic fits and convulsions in children.

Barbiturates are also thought to act on the GABA receptors, increasing their sensitivity. These are often prescribed to reduce the liability of epileptic siezures (Maksay and Ticku, 1985). Withdrawal from taking barbiturates should be gradual or results could be fatal.

Alcohol is a nonprescribed drug that also acts on the GABA receptors but is thought to act on different sites from barbiturates, because the effect of the two is cumulative and can prove fatal. Alcohol not only produces an anxiety-reducing effect through the GABA receptors, which is depressant in CNS terms, but encourages a release of dopamine, which is reinforcing. Alcohol addiction is of course a complex process; its social acceptability, or even encouragement, makes it difficult to separate out its clinical effects. In addition, there is thought to be a genetic component to alcohol addiction (reviewed by Cloninger, 1987). This may well be true for other drugs not yet researched in this way.

Neuroleptics

Also called 'major tranquillisers', this group of drugs is used in severe psychological or neurological disturbance.

One chemical group in this category is the **phenothiazines**. Phenothiazines act on the dopamine neurones and thereby reduce the activity of dopamine. These drugs were originally produced to reduce anxiety before a patient's operation, but were found to be so relaxing that their psychiatric possibilities were explored. They were found to be effective for reducing the hallucinations and other disturbances in schizophrenia and other severe mental states. Drugs in this group include chlorpromazine (Largactil) and the butyrophenones (for example haloperidol). Long-term use of these drugs has been criticised because of side-effects and a build-up of chemicals in the brain.

Stimulants

Stimulants are mood-lifting drugs, which increase alertness and feelings of self-confidence. The **amphetamines** (for example Dexadrine) fall into this category; they act by blocking the reuptake of dopamine and norepinephrine, which means that these neurotransmitters exert their excitatory influence for longer. They are potentially highly addictive. There is the likelihood that dopamine is one of the reinforcement mechanisms in the CNS.

FIGURE 3.12
Summary table of the action of some psychotrophic drugs

Effect group	Chemical group and examples	Neurochemical affected	Effect on mood or behaviour
Minor tranquillisers	Benzodiazepines (e.g. Librium, Valium)	Enhanced release of GABA (inhibitory)	Calming effect, reduce anxiety
Neuroleptics (antipsychotics)	Phenothiazines (e.g. chlorpromazine) Butyrophenones (haloperidol)	Dopamine – drug occupies receptors	Reduce psychotic experiences and strange motor movements
Stimulants	Amphetamines (Dexadrine)	Block reuptake of dopamine and norepinephrine	Increase alertness and feelings of confidence
Antidepressants	(1) Tricyclic antidepressants (2) Monoamine oxidase inhibitors	(1) Block breakdown of norepinephrine and serotonin (2) Block action of enzyme MAO, thus enhancing action of norepinephrine and serotonin	Produce lifted mood and feelings of euphoria, block REM sleep
Opiates	Morphine	Mimic action of endorphins	Soothing, calming, pain-reducing

Other drugs that prompt the release of dopamine are cocaine, nicotine and caffeine. Again, all are potentially addictive, although there are psychological as well as physical factors involved in these processes of addiction. Nicotine may be regarded as socially desirable, especially by youngsters, or as a token of rebellion. Caffeine is a socially acceptable way of 'getting a quick lift', and cocaine is present in some pain-relieving agents.

L-dopa, as mentioned earlier, is administered as treatment for Parkinson's disease. It enhances the levels of dopamine by providing the precursor for its synthesis in the brain.

Antidepressants

These may be prescribed for recognised clinical depression. There are two main chemical groups: (a) monoamine oxidase (MAO) inhibitors, and (b) tricyclic antidepressants.

MAO inhibitors

These drugs do exactly what the name implies: they inhibit, or interfere with, the enzyme (MAO) that destroys norepinephrine. Because of this action, norepinephrine circulates for longer, maintaining its excitatory effect. As mentioned earlier, the enzyme MAO is present in the bloodstream, where it deactivates food enzymes such as those found in cheese and chocolate. Patients taking these drugs must avoid those foods, or they could be subject to a damaging rise in blood pressure, through suppression of the enzyme.

Tricyclic antidepressants

Tricyclic antidepressants inhibit the reuptake of both serotonin and norepinephrine, thus prolonging the excitatory activity of both neurotransmitters.

Broadly, tricyclics fall into two categories:

1. those which are sedative, such as amytriptyline (Tryptizol), which benefit patients whose depression is accompanied by anxiety;

2. those which are nonsedative, such as **imipramine** (Tofranil), which benefit patients who become withdrawn and apathetic when depressed.

Other antidepressants

Other antidepressant drugs may act on other specific neurotransmitters. For example, Fluoxetine (better known as **Prozac**) is classed as an SSRI (specific serotonin re-uptake inhibitor) which effectively means that it prolongs the availability of that neurotransmitter.

Opiates

These are drugs that are prescribed for the control of strong pain. They include the medical version of opium, which is **morphine**, chemically the same as heroin. These drugs are highly addictive. They act on the opiate receptor sites normally used by the endorphins and enkephalins. If used regularly, they depress the individual's own production of endorphins. If the drug is withdrawn, the individual not only suffers the withdrawal symptoms that accompany the loss of any drug, such as nicotine, but also has reduced pain-modulating capacity, due to the low level of natural endorphins. Naturally, the clinical administration of opiate drugs is carefully controlled and monitored.

Other psychoactive drugs

We hear a great deal nowadays about nonprescribed psychoactive drugs and 'designer' drugs, which are mixes of known psychoactive substances, all of which are active in the brain, usually at neurotransmitter level. Undoubtedly, altering the chemical balance of the brain always has its dangers, whether done clinically or experimentally, as the young sufferers of Parkinson's disease (previously mentioned) would doubtless testify. Impurities and injudicious 'mixes' are probably the most harmful, but the problems of addiction and how to break the cycle, and how not to pass the addiction to one's children, given there may be a genetic component, are all problems as yet insoluble.

LSD (lysergic diethylamide acid) appears to stimulate certain of the serotonin receptors; the hallucinations that occur have been likened to 'dreaming while you are awake'. Of course, dreams can be pleasant or frightening, and as yet no one has satisfactorily explained the mechanism whereby the hallucinations reoccur even when the individual is not on the drug. LSD does not seem as addictive as was originally thought, but this is probably situation dependent.

We hear about 'exercise addicts' who are apparently 'high' on the catecholamines produced during exercise and who suffer withdrawal symptoms if their exercise is curtailed. How well researched the syndrome is remains to be seen, but the body does adapt upwards – or downwards – to changed chemical levels.

Curare is a drug that was synthesised from plants by the South American Indians as a poison with which to tip their arrows. Curare occupies the nicotinic receptor sites used by the neurotransmitter acetylcholine, which effectively blocks the neuromuscular junction, causing paralysis. Consciousness is not affected. In modern times, a form of curare was used during operations as a muscle relaxant, so that muscles would not contract during surgery. In addition, an anaesthetic needs to be used (so that the patient is not conscious and does not feel the pain of the scalpel), together with a respirator to compensate for lack of tone in the respiratory muscles.

Summary

Psychoactive drugs generally exert their influence at the synapse, by either imitating or blocking the action of a specific neurotransmitter (see Figure 3.12). Mood changes may be brought about in this way. Many psychoactive drugs are addictive, and some also depress the body's own natural production of chemicals.

Self-assessment questions

1. Describe how the minor tranquillisers act on the human brain.
2. Which psychoactive drugs act on the dopamine circuit, and with what effect?
3. Briefly describe two main types of antidepressant.
4. Describe the action and consequences of opiates.

SECTION V   THE AUTONOMIC NERVOUS SYSTEM

The ANS is the part of the peripheral nervous system that is concerned with the regulation of internal structures: smooth muscle, heart muscle and glands. Smooth muscle is found in the intestines, bowel, bladder, blood vessels, skin (around hair follicles) and eyes (controlling pupil size and accommodation of the lens).

'Autonomic' means self-controlling or self-regulating; as you can see from this list, most of the structures mentioned are controlled without our conscious intervention, with the exception of bladder and bowel, which we learn to control at an early age. This should imply that we could learn to control our heart rate and blood pressure, but few of us do. A technique called biofeedback has been taught to some patients suffering from high blood pressure. They were connected to apparatus that constantly monitored blood pressure and were asked to concentrate on lowering their blood pressure to an acceptable level. When this was reached, a tone sounded. This was the only reinforcement they needed, plus of course the knowledge that they were improving their health. Unfortunately, the improvement was not maintained once they were disconnected from the apparatus.

The ANS consists of two separate systems, the **sympathetic division** and the **parasympathetic division**, both of which have nerve connections to most internal organs. The two divisions act like two ends of a see-saw: when one end is 'up', the other is 'down'. Both cannot be active and in control of the body at the same time, as they often have opposing effects on the same organ (see Figure 3.13).

The ANS works in close conjunction with the **endocrine system**, another of the body's systems that is not under conscious control (see Chapter 4). Activities of the ANS are co-ordinated by the hypothalamus and the limbic system. These links can be seen to be important as the hypothalamus also effectively controls the endocrine system, because of its close links to the pituitary gland. The limbic system is involved in emotional responses, which also need the involvement of the ANS.

FIGURE 3.13
Actions of the ANS on organs of the body

Structure	Sympathetic action	Parasympathetic action
Heart	Increases rate	Resting rate
Blood vessels	Dilates	Contracts
Pupils	Dilates	Contracts
Gut*	Slows movement	Speeds movement
Salivary glands	Decreases production	Maintains production
Bronchi (lungs)	Dilates (aids breathing)	Resting state
Adrenal glands	Stimulates	Resting state
Liver	Releases glucose	Stores glucose
GSR**	Decreases	Increases
Bladder, bowel	Relaxed	Toned
Skin (a) Hair follicle	Erected	Relaxed
(b) Capillaries	Dilated (blushing)	Contracted

* The action of the Sympathetic Division may here seem the opposite to your own observation; when experiencing a strong emotion such as fear, you may have noticed a churning feeling in the stomach ('butterflies'). This is due to a parasympathetic surge, before the sympathetic takes over. Sometimes you go as far as emptying the bladder or bowel. Once you become embroiled in your fight, or other activity, 'butterflies' cease as the sympathetic is in control.

** GSR: This stands for galvanic skin response. It is a measure of the electrical resistance of the skin. This is decreased by sweating, when the skin gets wet; it is associated with anxiety-provoking situations, such as fear or anger, and other strong emotions such as love, hate and passion. This is the process used by lie-detector machines – notoriously unreliable, as good spies are trained to control their autonomic responses!

The sympathetic division

This division becomes more active when the individual becomes active. Imagine this situation: You are walking down the high street when you see a lion. You have the choice of running away or staying to fight. Your CNS will make the conscious decision for you, but your ANS has already become mobilised, without needing conscious instruction. Whichever alternative is chosen, activity is the order of the day; therefore the sympathetic speeds up the heart rate (remember that nerve impulses take only split seconds to travel), dilates the walls of the blood vessels to speed blood to the limbs, dilates the pupils so that you can see your adversary more clearly, releases glucose into the bloodstream for energy, and brings other changes into play that are advantageous for an active state (see Figure 3.1). The actions of the ANS are reinforced by the activity of the endocrine system; sympathetic nerves also directly stimulate the adrenal glands to release adrenaline.

When all danger is past, the parasympathetic division takes over to restore the body's balance.

The parasympathetic division

This is the division of the ANS which seeks to conserve the body's resources. It prompts salivation and gastric movements, including peristalsis (the movement of food through the small intestine), and encourages blood flow to the gastrointestinal system and storage of glucose by the liver.

SUMMARY

The ANS mobilises and integrates the body's physiological responses to changes of situation and mood, without the individual's conscious intervention. There are strong links with the CNS and the endocrine system. The two divisions of the ANS both send axons to the same areas of the body, but these two systems do not take action at the same time. The sympathetic division mobilises the body's energetic responses, while the parasympathetic division controls the conserving mode of the body.

SELF-ASSESSMENT QUESTIONS

1. What effects does the sympathetic division of the ANS have on major organs or structures of the body?
2. What are the advantages to the individual of sympathetic changes in heart rate, blood pressure and other specific effects?
3. Why is the parasympathetic division of the ANS necessary?

FURTHER READING

S. Springer and G. Deutsch, *Left Brain, Right Brain* (San Francisco: Freeman, 1985).

N.R. Carlson, *Physiology of Behaviour* (Boston, Mass.: Allyn & Bacon, 1991).

J.G. Beaumont, *Understanding Neuropsychology* (Oxford: Blackwell, 1988).

The Endocrine System

By the end of this chapter you will be able to:

- describe the organisation of the endocrine system;
- outline the functions of the glands in the system;
- understand how the actions of hormones influence behaviour; and
- discuss the interaction of the endocrine system and the nervous system.

INTRODUCTION

The endocrine system is a system of glands and their secretions that act within the body. The human body is under the control not only of the nervous system, but also of a complementary system of hormones (chemicals), which are released by specialised neurones or glands into the bloodstream or other areas of the body. These are released in response to situations or impulses or the normal cycles of the body, and are not usually a product of conscious control, but are regulated automatically by the body itself. Their action is effectively much slower than that of the nervous system, but their effect is longer lasting, as the chemicals will continue circulating until they are broken down by the body. The pituitary gland is often called the 'master gland' as it directs the activities of many other glands in the body.

89

SECTION I   THE PITUITARY GLAND

Although the pituitary gland is situated within the cranium, it is part of the endocrine system rather than the nervous system. However, as you would expect from its siting, it has very close links with the nervous system. The hypothalamus, the brain structure next to the pituitary, exerts a great deal of control over the endocrine system. It has some **neurosecretory cells** that manufacture hormones to be released directly into the bloodstream serving the **anterior pituitary** (see Figure 4.1). This prompts the anterior pituitary to secrete its hormones and release them at the appropriate time. Some of these hormones are briefly described below.

Anterior pituitary hormones

1. **Growth hormone** is released steadily throughout childhood, with an extra 'spurt' during adolescence (prompting the concurrent growth spurt). This is terminated in girls by the onset of menstruation, and in boys, by the increased production of testosterone.
2. **Gonadotrophic hormone** controls the production of the male and female sex hormones by prompting the appropriate sex glands (testes in males and ovaries in females) to produce their hormones.
3. **Thyrotrophic hormone** prompts the thyroid gland to secrete thyroxin, which controls the body's metabolic rate (the rate at which the body uses up food for fuel, in order to produce activity).
4. **Prolactin** prompts the production of milk in pregnant and nursing mothers.
5. **Adrenocorticotrophic hormone** (ACTH for short!) signals to the adrenal glands to produce their secretions; this is sometimes referred to as the 'stress' or 'activity' response.

Posterior pituitary hormones

The hormones of the **posterior pituitary** are actually manufactured in the hypothalamus but stored in the posterior pituitary. The instruction to release them into the bloodstream also comes from the hypothalamus. These hormones are:

- **oxytocin,** the hormone that controls the release of milk and the contraction of the uterus during childbirth; and
- **vasopressin,** or antidiuretic hormone, which regulates the output of urine by the kidneys.

FIGURE 4.1
Hormones of the pituitary gland

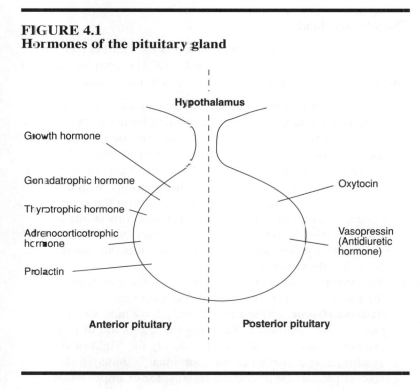

SECTION II OTHER GLANDS IN THE HUMAN ENDOCRINE SYSTEM

Glands are situated throughout the body (see Figure 4.2); each has a specific role or activity and produces its own specific secretions.

Having briefly outlined the actions of the pituitary gland, it is now possible to look at the activity of some of the other glands that are relevant to the purpose of this book. Of course, all glands have bearing not only on the body but also on the mental state of the individual, but it is outside the scope of this book to discuss them all. However, certain are of paramount importance to the understanding of overt behaviour and will be mentioned here.

The adrenal glands

These sit like three-cornered hats on top of the kidneys (see Figure 4.2). Their secretions are prompted by ACTH from the anterior pituitary gland. There are two active parts to the adrenal gland:

1. The **adrenal medulla** (the central area of the gland) secretes **adrenaline** and **noradrenaline**, needed by the body to assist physical activites. Both of these hormones are involved in the 'fight or flight' syndrome (discussed in Chapter 3), which is mediated by the ANS. They also have a role to play in the physiological processes of the emotions, which we shall look at in Chapter 5. Adrenaline acts on the heart muscle, prompting the heart to beat faster; this is one reason why atheletes 'psych themselves up': they promote a flow of adrenaline by psychological means which is then used by the body for physical purposes.
2. The **adrenal cortex**, the outer layers of the gland, produces the **corticosteroids**, for example **cortisol** and **hydrocortisone**, utilised by the body for a number of physiological purposes, including the regulation of blood pressure. This is called into play during the 'fight or flight' syndrome, and also when the individual is under stress. Excess production of corticosteroids, for example when an individual is under constant stress, is detrimental to the body, because of the hypertension (raised blood pressure) and other physical changes they promote.

The pancreas

Cells in the pancreas produce insulin, which prompts the cells in the liver to break down glucose (simple sugar) for use by the body, or for storage as glycogen by the liver. The pancreas releases its insulin according to how much sugar has been ingested and how much exercise the person has taken to burn up th∋ sugar. Diabetics (with diabetes mellitus) do not produce enough insulin for this process and have to inject themselves with insulin to 'top up' their own supply. They become adept at gauging how much insulin they need, bearing in mind their exercise/food balance (because all carbohydrates consumed are converted to sugar by the body).

FIGURE 4.2
Some of the endocrine glands

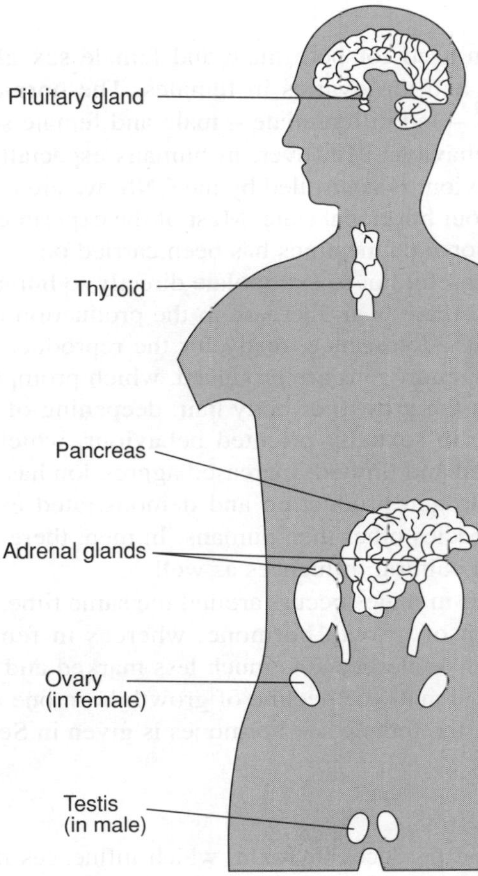

Pituitary gland

Thyroid

Pancreas

Adrenal glands

Ovary
(in female)

Testis
(in male)

However, injected insulin is released into the body on a regular timescale, rather than according to need, as is naturally occurring insulin, and diabetics who miss meals, or who are subject to physical or mental stress, may lapse into an insulin coma. Warning behaviours for this may include unprovoked anger, irritation or aggressiveness, because the brain is the first organ to respond behaviourally to a lack of sugar. You yourself may have noticed you feel bad-tempered if you have not eaten for some time. An injection of a glucose solution quickly resolves an insulin coma.

The gonads

This is the term used for both male and female sex glands: the testes in males and the ovaries in females. The hormones they produce govern – and differentiate – male and female sexual and reproductive behaviour. However, in humans especially, a great deal of the behaviour is controlled by the CNS; we are not entirely at the mercy of our hormonal state. Most of the experimental work on neural–hormonal connections has been carried out on animals, so we must be careful not to extrapolate directly to humans.

In both sexes, there is an increase in the production of the sex hormones during adolescence, ready for the reproductive period of life. In males, androgens are produced, which prompt physical changes such as the growth of body hair, deepening of the voice and an increase in sexually oriented behaviour, which is often culturally defined and limited. Increased aggression has also been linked with androgen production and demonstrated experimentally in many species other than humans. In men, there are likely to be neural and cultural influences as well.

A growth spurt in males occurs around the same time, owing to extra production of growth hormone, whereas in females, the growth pattern in adolescence is much less marked and the onset of menstruation signals the decline of growth hormone secretion. A description of the female sex hormones is given in Section IV.

The thyroid

The thyroid gland produces thyroxin, which influences the body's metabolic rate (the rate at which the body uses up food to produce energy). This influences behaviour in that an over production of thyroxin accelerates metabolic rate, causing the individual to become highly active, jumpy and 'nervy', which is coupled with weight loss. Underproduction of thyroxin leads to lethargy and weight gain.

The pineal gland

In lower vertebrates such as sharks, frogs and lizards, the pineal gland detects changes in levels of illumination; hence it is often referred to as the 'third eye'. In humans, it secretes a hormone called **melatonin** which is synthesised from serotonin. Melatonin is influential in the body's **circadian rhythms**, the daily cycle of sleeping and waking activities (more of this in Chapter 7). Sugden *et al.* (1985) suggest that there is complex biochemical control of circadian rhythms, involving chemicals manufactured by the pineal gland.

Other glands in the human body

There are other glands in the human body that produce secretions rather than hormones, for example the salivary glands, which are the first step in the chemical digestive chain of events. As mentioned in the previous chapter, the salivary glands are linked to the ANS, and the production of saliva is suspended in strong emotional states such as fear. Another gland that produces secretions rather than hormones, but is linked to the reproductive cycle, is the prostate in males. This is a gland very rarely mentioned, yet it has an important function; it manufactures the seminal fluid that surrounds the sperm. Probably because so few men realise they have a prostate gland, cancers of the prostate are often ignored until too late. By and large, glands that produce secretions, rather than hormones, do not have such a direct influence on behaviour as do the hormone-producing glands.

SECTION III ENDOCRINE LINKS WITH THE NERVOUS SYSTEM

Links with the CNS

The most obvious link between the endocrine system and the CNS is that the hypothalamus controls the pituitary gland; as this in turn orchestrates most of the other glands, endocrine control can be traced back to the hypothalamus. There is feedback from hormonal levels to the CNS that determines whether glands are then prompted to release or cease production of further hormones. This link is often called the HPA (hypothalamus-pituitary axis).

Links with the ANS

The ANS prompts the release of adrenaline from the adrenal glands in strong emotional states and when there is a need for increased physical activity. The ANS also influences metabolic rate, through the thyroid gland.

Links with the PNS

The skeletal system is linked directly to the CNS to perform voluntary movements, through the PNS, which sends out impulses along axons to the limbs. However, there are hormonal influences involved, through both the production of adrenaline and, to a lesser extent, the activity of the thyroid and pancreas. When overt activity is inappropriate or impossible, the restless pacing up and down of a frustrated or disturbed individual characterises the PNS/endocrine link.

SECTION IV INTERACTIONAL EFFECTS WITH BEHAVIOUR

The endocrine and nervous systems, it can be seen, do not function in isolation but as an intergrated whole. External stimuli are recognised and sorted by the CNS, which activates the ANS and endocrine systems to change the internal environment, and the PNS is then brought in as the **effector**, to carry out whatever needs to be done. Alternatively, if the internal state of the body changes through anxiety or hormonal imbalance rather than the perception of external stimuli, feedback from the hormonal levels activates the CNS and ANS, and frequently the PNS as well, in either effective or ineffective actions.

In effect, we have three systems that interact:

1 *Mechanical.* Skeletal and muscular processes are necessary for the expression of overt behaviour – remember that even speech is overt behaviour and requires muscle and bone movement.
2 *Chemical.* The endocrine function controls hormonal chemical messengers, which are circulated in the bloodstream.
3. *Neural.* The mechanisms of the nervous system are capable of complex and modifiable action. They can learn by experience and adapt to changes in the environment.

Reactions to environmental stimuli

Changes in the environment that are perceived by the individual to be relevant or important set off a chain of activity, which needs to be completed in order to restore the individual's equilibrium (see Figure 4.3).

External stimuli are recognised by the CNS, and the ANS is alerted. This prompts appropriate hormonal change to occur, which assists the nervous system in sustaining the behaviour already instigated (hormonal changes are slower to start but as a rule, of sustained duration). If you were crossing the road and a car blew its horn at you (**external stimulus**), you would recognise the sound (**CNS activity**) and skip promptly onto the pavement (**PNS activity, instructed by CNS**). At the same time, your ANS has been alerted to deal with this emergency, which has brought in the endocrine system; adrenaline is released into your bloodstream, which takes a little while to circulate. This explains why, after you are safely on the pavement, your heart starts thumping and your knees feel like jelly (**hormonal change**)!

FIGURE 4.3
Reactions of the nervous and endocrine systems to enviromental stimuli

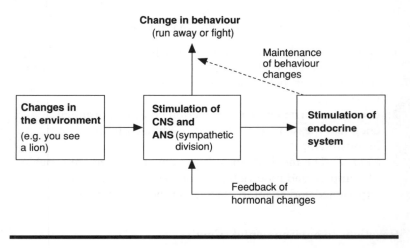

Reactions to internal changes

Changes in the internal environment of the body may be brought about for a variety of reasons: changes in emotional state, malfunction due to illness or cyclical changes. An example of a cyclical occurrence is menstruation.

The menstrual cycle and its effect on behaviour

The **menstrual cycle**, of approximately 28 days in the human female, encompasses a number of hormonal changes, often paralleled by behavioural changes. In some cases, the physical and behavioural effects of these changes are unpleasant, to say the least; this has been termed **premenstrual syndrome** (PMS). There has been some debate as to whether the syndrome exists as a physical entity or whether it is 'all in the mind', as some suggest. Who is to judge?

Menstruation is marked by the uterus shedding its lining and associated blood vessels. As mentioned above, the reproductive cycle involves a sequence of hormonal events, controlled by the pituitary. Gonadotrophic hormones, especially **follicle-stimulating hormone** (FSH) from the anterior pituitary, stimulate the growth of ovarian follicles, cells surrounding each ovum. The ovum or egg cells are present in every female from birth, but need to be developed before being passed into the uterus for fertilisation. Usually, one is released each month; if two are released and fertilised, they will grow into dizygotic (non-identical) twins.

The maturing follicle secrets **oestradiol**, one of the female cycle hormones. As the level of this hormone rises to a peak, there is a rise in the secretion of **luteinising hormone** (LH). This causes ovulation to occur, the ovum is released into the uterus and the follicle ruptures, becoming a **corpus luteum**, producing oestradiol and **progesterone**, both hormones that prepare the uterus for pregnancy by maintaining the lining and also prevent the ovaries producing another follicle. If the ovum is not fertilised, the production of oestradiol and progesterone ceases and the lining of the uterus is shed.

Figure 4.4 shows the relative timespan of these hormonal activities.

Behavioural changes associated with these changes in hormonal levels are often a point for argument, but it is usually agreed that increased sexual activity corresponds with the 'peaks' associated with oestradiol and LH, while high progesterone levels, which would normally be maintained throughout pregnancy, indicate a slowing of generally active behaviour.

In addition to these fluctuating behaviour patterns, a number of women complain of increased fluid retention in PMS, giving a 'bloated' feeling at the progesterone peak and for some days into menstruation. It has been suggested by some studies (reviewed by Floody, 1983) that aggressive behaviours are more likely to occur shortly before the onset of menstruation. Others suggest that imbalance of progesterone/oestradiol is marked by aggressive or antisocial behaviours, such as shoplifting. Restoration of the hormonal balance by the administration of one or other of the hormones, usually progesterone, has had excellent results in changing behaviour. If hormonal imbalance is at the basis of PMS, it is understandable why only some, and not all, women suffer from it, and some for only part of their reproductive lives. As a syndrome, it should not be rejected out of hand, especially by those who have never experienced it. It can be as real, as complex and as distressing as male impotence!

FIGURE 4.4
Relative amounts of sex hormones in the bloodstream throughout a 28-day menstrual cycle

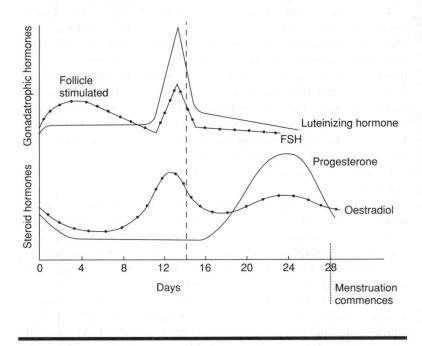

SUMMARY

The activity of most endocrine glands is prompted by hormones from the pituitary gland, which is itself under the control of the hypothalamus, a subcortical brain structure. Hormones secreted by the endocrine glands are as essential as the nervous system in integrating human activity; harmonious interaction of neural, chemical and skeletal systems is important for coherent, balanced activity. While nerve impulses can travel through the body in a fraction of a second, hormones are much slower to reach their target site, requiring seconds if not minutes. However, the action of hormones is sustained for as long as the chemicals continue to circulate in the body.

SELF-ASSESSMENT QUESTIONS

1. (a) List the hormones produced by the anterior pituitary.
   (b) Which further hormones are prompted by each of these?
2. What behaviour changes are attributable to these hormones?
3. How does the activity of the endocrine system integrate with that of the nervous system?

FURTHER READING

G. M. Shepherd, *Neurobiology*. (Oxford: Oxford University Press, 1988).

Okay, okay — I say "Lack of non-homeostatic motivation" — you say "Lazy" ...

Motivation and Emotion

By the end of this chapter you will be able to:

● distinguish between examples of homeostatic and nonhomeostatic motivation;
● understand the physiological basis of emotion, and the psychological recognition of emotions in the self and others; and
● compare and contrast a number of theories of emotion.

INTRODUCTION

Motivation is an issue at the heart of psychology; why do people behave as they do? Why does behaviour take one form and not another? And what makes people behave differently from – or similarly to – each other?

In this chapter, we have linked motivation and emotion, as these two phenomena are often linked in real life. If you feel great fear (emotion), you are motivated to run away – although you may stay and fight instead; the resulting behaviours are not always what would be predicted from either the extent of the emotion or the situation. This is what makes the study of motivation and emotion so complex and interesting.

Atkinson *et al.* (1985) suggest that, while motives are internally caused, emotion is a response to an external stimulus. In this chapter, we will examine both motivation and emotion; see if you agree with their assertion at the end.

103

SECTION I   HOMEOSTATIC MOTIVATION

'**Homeostasis**' is a term that was first used by the physiologist Cannon in the 1920s, to describe the process through which the body's balanced state is maintained (see Figure 5.1). Homeostasis has been recognised as one factor in the motivation of human behaviour.

WHAT DOES HOMEOSTASIS ACHIEVE?

Most homeostatic mechanisms are controlled automatically, by the ANS and the endocrine system (described in the last two chapters), and the hypothalamus, which is the structure in the CNS linking the autonomic and endocrine systems. Blood pressure, heart rate, temperature, chemical balance inside and outside the body's cells, levels of oxygen and carbon dioxide in the blood, digestion, respiration and hormonal balance – all these are regulated without conscious effort on the part of the individual.

Sensations of hunger or thirst are produced autonomically and raised to our conscious awareness; the final act of eating or drinking is due to a conscious decision; that is to say, the motivation arises homeostatically (involuntarily) but the resulting consumatory behaviour is voluntary. The motivation of eating behaviour is a complex and interesting area of study, and one which also demonstrates that homeostatic mechanisms are not the whole answer to why people behave as they do.

Motivation for eating

How do you know that you are hungry? What is your **subjective experience** that motivates you to seek out food? You may have an 'empty' feeling in the upper abdomen, stomach rumbling noises, feelings of weakness or even a headache, or a combination of factors. Physiologists have found that there are several factors that signal and cause an animal to find food.

The immediate signal

The first signal may be the absence of food in the stomach.

Cannon and Washburn (1912) investigated this probability; Washburn swallowed a balloon that could be inflated within his stomach, and the researchers found that the contractions of the stomach coincided with reported feelings of hunger. When the balloon was inflated, the contractions no longer took place.

FIGURE 5.1
Diagrammatic representation of homeostasis

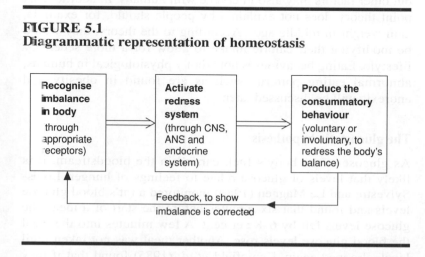

Neural factors

Since many ANS functions are controlled from the hypothalamus in the brain, it seemed reasonable to search for some type of 'control centre' there. Hetherington and Ransom (1942) and Anand and Brobeck (1951) claimed to have identified areas of the hypothalamus that promoted feeding behaviour (in the lateral hypothalamus area, LHA) and an adjacent satiation centre (in the ventromedial hypothalamus, VMH), which cuts off feeding behaviour when the individual is sated. Certainly, the hypothalamus is involved in feeding behaviour, but it is not the sole area of control.

Set point theory

Identification of the influence of these two areas of the hypothalamus brought forward the suggestion that a balance obtained between the two would result in an individual's body weight set point. **Set point theory** suggests that individuals will eat to maintain their own body weight. This seemed like a useful explanation for why slimmers only succeed for a while and then go back to their previous weight. Set point theory has been demonstrated experimentally with rats (for example Keesey and Powley, 1975), but other factors may also intervene with humans. In addition, set point theory does not explain why people should, for example, gain weight in middle age. According to the theory, they would be modifying their calorie intake to allow for a more sedentary lifestyle. Eating behaviour is not wholly physiological in humans; abnormal eating patterns such as are found in obesity and anorexia will be discussed later.

The glucostatic hypothesis

As glucose is the body's fuel, carried in the bloodstream, it is likely that levels of glucose relate to feelings of hunger. Louis-Sylvestre and Le Magnen (1980) monitored a rat's blood glucose levels and found that six minutes before the start of a meal, the glucose levels fell by 6–8 per cent. A few minutes into the meal the blood glucose levels rose. Another meal was not taken until levels dropped again. Campfield *et al.* (1985) found that if they injected a small amount of glucose into the rat, the meal was postponed by the animal, as if the hunger signal was removed. We can relate this to human behaviour: if you feel hungry and eat a chocolate bar (containing sugar, which needs little transformation to glucose), you may find that you no longer feel hungry, and may then choose to delay or miss a meal. Bellisle *et al.* (1984) found that people who skip breakfast have lower blood glucose levels at lunchtime, and consequently tend to eat more lunch!

Glucose receptors

How does the body monitor its glucose levels? In the blood vessels, the brain (hypothalamus) and other organs of the body are **glucose receptors**, neurones that detect the amount of glucose present in the body. If the level drops and no food is available, more glucose is released from the liver, which is the body's storehouse for glycogen (the storable form of glucose).

Investigations have shown that glucose receptors in the hypothalamus are not the primary and most important signal for low glucose levels and initiating feeding. Even when the hypothalamus is damaged, feeding behaviour follows a regular pattern.

Russek (1971) demonstrated the importance of the glucose receptors in the liver. He injected glucose into the hepatic portal vein of a dog (a vein that carries blood from the intestines to the liver). This injection caused the dog to stop eating and induced long-term satiety, whereas a similar injection into the jugular vein, in the neck, carrying glucose around the body, had little effect on eating behaviour.

There appears to be an interactional effect between hepatic and hypothalamic receptors. Shimizu *et al.* (1983) found that the response firing rate of detectors in the hypothalamus was reduced when glucose was injected close to the liver. This would seem to suggest a linkage between the two systems; in the absence of one, hunger can be evoked by the other.

Social and environmental factors

Certainly for humans, meals, from grand banquets to having a sandwich at lunchtime with a friend, are often social occasions. We also tend to eat more at a meal when in company. De Castro and de Castro (1989) asked subjects to keep a food diary for seven days, not only of what they ate, but also of with whom they ate it. Subsequent analysis showed that when in company, subjects ate more. In addition, they also found that, although people stated that they would usually eat one large meal and one small meal per day, this rule no longer held; meal sizes related only to company rather than to the size of the previous meal.

Incentives to eat

The sight or smell of attractive food is also an incentive for humans to eat. Salivary glands are stimulated by the sight – or even the thought – of attractive food. A dish of strawberries or an attractive cake might encourage many people to eat, although they had not previously felt hungry.

Routine

Humans are also 'trained' to expect to eat meals at regular times. If you are absorbed in a task, you may not feel hungry. On catching sight of the clock, you may realise it is past your regular mealtime and hurry to get something to eat. Expectancy plays a role in human feeding behaviour.

Flavours

Sweet flavours, as shown in Chapter 2, are recognised by the tongue as pleasant and palatable. Brala and Hagen (1983) demonstrated that sweet flavours actually make subjects feel hungrier and can encourage further intake of food.

Humans thrive on a varied and wide-ranging diet, unlike some animals, for example koalas, who only eat eucalyptus leaves. If we ate only one food constantly, we would certainly become tired of it. Rolls *et al.* (1981) found that people would eat a larger meal if they were offered four different types of sandwich filling.

Summary

Physiological factors involved in the motivation of eating behaviour include the detection of reduced glucose levels in the body by receptors in the liver, the hypothalamus and the circulatory system. Satiety is signalled by the hypothalamus before the ingested meal is digested, or overeating would result. Psychological factors that prompt eating include the sight or smell of attractive food, the availability of a variety of foods, company for a meal and the prompting of the time of day.

EATING DISORDERS

These include obesity, anorexia nervosa and bulimia. The causes and treatments of these problems are still being investigated.

Obesity

There are certainly many different causes of obesity.

● Genetic or acquired physiological problems;

- faulty learning about eating behaviour; and
- psychological problems such as stress;

are all blamed.

Physiological problems

The hereditary basis to obesity was investigated by Stunkard *et al.* (1986), who found that the bodyweight of people who had been adopted was correlated with that of their biological parents but not of their adoptive parents. Other similar studies support the probability of a genetic factor in obesity.

Individuals vary in the efficiency of their metabolism. People with an efficient metabolism will gain weight on the same dietary intake as others with a less efficient metabolism, who may lose weight (Rodin *et al.*, 1989).

Dieting may in fact be detrimental to weight control in obese people. During the diet, weight is lost and the metabolism becomes more efficient, as a reaction to 'lean times'. Once the diet is stopped, the increased efficiency of the metabolism will produce an increase in weight, rather than a maintenance of the newer, slimmer person. No one has yet identified why some people have a more efficient metabolism than others.

Psychological problems

A range of psychological variables has been suggested to cause obesity:

- lack of oral gratification;
- food as a substitute for affection;
- lack of impulse control; and
- stress and/or depression.

Lack of oral gratification in infancy   This refers to Freudian theory, in which Freud suggested that lack of sucking time at the breast or bottle during the first stage of development led to a need in adulthood to seek oral gratification. Overeating could be regarded as an excessive psychological drive to put food in the mouth; however, some obese people consume no more food than others of normal body weight. In the same way, eating too fast is regarded as another possible indicator of lack of oral gratification in infancy. However, it is only a minority of obese people who eat too fast, as do some normal-weight people, so this can hardly be regarded as a major cause of obesity.

Food as a substitute for affection   Again this is a very intangible suggestion and one which is difficult to research. This idea may be approached in two ways:

1. A parent feels unable to give a child affection, for whatever reason, and gives gifts of food (sweets, biscuits, cakes) whenever the child appears to crave affection. Consequently, the child learns to respond to internal feelings of affection (motivation towards love) by eating.
2. A child or adult feels unable to give or receive love from others, and feels that they must love themselves; food is the expression of affection.

Both of these eventualities may have a circular effect, in that once the individual has put on weight, he or she sees himself or herself as unlovable by others and food as the self-consolation. Overweight adults were often overweight as childern.

Both of these positions have proved difficult to research, as they would necessarily involve **introspection**. This is a technique regarded as open to bias by the individual who is examining innermost thoughts and needs. Lack of appropriate methods are available for the measurement of intangible elements, such as the need for affection. How do you measure 'enough affection'?

Lack of impulse control   This explanation refers to a person's inability to control the desire to eat. It suggests that personality characteristics may be responsible for obesity. Lack of impulse control may be a general characteristic, applied to any behaviour, or specifically with regard to food consumption. This may be the case in overweight people, who see something they would like and eat it, with no regard for consequential weight gain.

This suggestion would seem to concur with physiological studies that suggest that people will eat more when attractive food is available. If this coincides with a personality deficiency of lack of control, the result may be obesity. However, this does not explain why the 'lack of control' is a characteristic present in some but not others, and why it should be specifically directed at food in some people.

Stress and/or depression   People under stress, and people who are depressed, may react by eating more than usual, especially sweet foods (comfort foods, as they have been called). This may have the effect of making the individual put on weight. It has also been suggested that, while depressed, people may cease to care about their appearance, and therefore do not aim to maintain a pleasing body outline – whether this is a conscious decision or not has yet to be demonstrated.

Conversely, many stressed or depressed people in fact lose weight, having little interest in food as a substitute or even as a means of self-maintenance. Others may not find their appetite or body weight affected at all.

Overview

Rodin and her colleagues (1989) reviewed the literature on some of the causes suggested above and found very little empirical support for any of them. In fact, unhappiness and depression seemed more likely to be the effects rather than the causes of obesity.

Obesity, like the motivation for eating, appears to be multifactorial. A number of physiological or psychological factors may be involved, in any combination, for any one individual. The process of identifying these could be extremely time-consuming and probably tedious for the individual concerned. This is why obesity is very difficult to treat successfully.

Anorexia nervosa

This is a life-threatening problem, predominantly Western-world based and mainly affecting adolescents; it is 20 times more common in girls than boys. The individual refuses to eat or eats only minimal amounts, resulting in extreme weight loss. Causes put forward include those that are:

- social;
- cultural;
- emotional; and
- physiological.

Social causes

Learning theorists suggest the sufferers are trying to emulate the slim models so valued by Western society. In order to look like a model, the young girl refuses to eat in order to lose weight, but fails to recognise when her body outline has gone beyond slim, to gaunt.

Family conflict has also been suggested as a cause. Adolescence, it has been suggested, is often a time of rebellion against parental values or control. The anorexic adolescent may feel unable to rebel openly, but the refusal of food takes the place of rebellion. Alternatively, other members of the family may be in conflict, parents with each other or other siblings. If this conflict cannot be brought out into the open and resolved, the conflict is deflected on to the sufferer's 'disease'. The family is often a family of 'achievers', and it has been suggested the anorexic individual may feel inadequate.

Cultural causes

Certainly most anorexics have a distorted body image; they see themselves as 'fat', while seeing others of the same dimensions as 'thin'. Body image is culturally defined. Some cultures expect women to be fatter than other cultures' expectations. Even within Europe, there are cultural variations.

Emotional causes

Psychoanalytic theorists suggest that the sufferer equates food with sexual love, and refusal of food is a rejection of sexuality. The desire to retain a small body may be the expression of the wish to remain a child. In severe cases of anorexia, menstruation ceases, which supports the wish to revert to childhood and deny sexuality.

Anorexics are not disinterested in food. Some spend a great deal of time collecting recipes and cooking meals for others but will then not partake, saying they are 'not hungry'.

Physiological correlates

As a result of severe weight loss in females, menstruation ceases, and the stored ova may be damaged, depleted or reabsorbed. Osteoporosis and subsequent bone fractures are common.

Artmann *et al.* (1985) reported that CT scans of anorexic patients revealed changes in the brain: widened sulci and enlarged ventricles. Suggestions that anorexia may be caused by structural or biochemical abnormalities in the brain mechanisms controlling metabolism or eating behaviour have been investigated by researchers. A literature review by Fava *et al.* (1989) evidenced changes in levels of norepinephrine, serotonin and opiods, but whether these are the cause or the result of anorexia has not been demonstrated.

A study by Broberg and Bernstein (1989) showed that, when presented with warm, appetising food (visual and olfactory stimulation), anorexic subjects produced more insulin in their bloodstream than did thin, nonanorexic subjects (the control group). Even so, the control group ate the food, while the anorexics did not, saying that they were not hungry. Learning theorists would suggest they find the symptoms of hunger reinforcing.

Treatments

Current treatments for anorexia include social, emotional and physiological treatments, but reports of success are not much more than over 50 per cent (for example Patton, 1989). Some anorexics have to be hospitalised and fed intravenously. Even with treatment, approximately one in 30 dies.

Bulimia

Bulimia involves the rejection of food followed by 'binges', during which the individual gorges, frequently on a particular type of food. This is usually followed by feelings of guilt, self-induced vomiting and the use of laxatives.

Sufferers from bulimia seldom lose as much weight, and rarely to such life-threatening proportions, as do anorexics. However, they often have an equal fear of obesity. The continual vomiting may have physiological consequences such as intestinal damage and nutritional deficiencies.

OTHER VIEWS OF HOMEOSTASIS

Many variations on the basic model of homeostasis have been produced; these attempt to explain not only the mechanisms instigating a behaviour, but also why the behaviour ceases. For example, a hungry animal will stop eating before the ingested food has been digested, raising blood glucose levels to 'full'. The basic model of homeostasis failed to explain why this occurs. In addition, the homeostatic model fails to explain the phenomenon of **feedforward**, observed by McFarland (1971). An animal will drink extra in anticipation of thirst, or eat more than usual in anticipation of a 'hungry' period. Simple cause-and-effect mechanisms are inadequate explanations for such motivated behaviour.

Summary

The body's homeostatic responses are largely involuntary, automatically controlled through the action of the **ANS**. You do not have to think, 'I am cold; I will produce goosepimples.' However, many of the behavioural responses to homeostatic motivations are voluntary, for example eating and drinking. Negative feedback cuts off the consummatory behaviour, but the precise mechanisms for this are not clearly understood.

Self-assessment questions

1. (a) What is meant by the term 'homeostasic motivation'?
   (b) Explain briefly how the body's internal systems are involved.
2. Describe the processes involved in one type of homeostatic behaviour.
3. Describe what happens when the system fails to operate
   (a) in motivating eating behaviour, and (b) in cutting off the eating behaviour.

SECTION II NONHOMEOSTATIC MOTIVATION

Homeostatic motivation can provide some explanation for life-sustaining behaviour. The same explanation does not hold for other motivated behaviours. These include:

- play;
- sexual behaviour;
- curiousity;
- gambling;
- addiction; and
- risk-taking;

Some of these can be seen as life-threatening rather than life-maintaining. Neural factors, hormonal factors and physiological mechanisms that feature in homeostatic motivation may contribute to these other forms of motivation, but not in the same way.

Curiosity and exploration

Many animals exhibit the motivation to explore their surroundings even when they are not pursuing specific goals such as food, drink or escape. Some also exhibit what can only be described as curiosity, for example watching others of the same or different species, or investigating objects that have no relevance to them (for example, having no odours that might indicate food). People, too, demonstrate curiosity, in varying degrees.

Blanchard *et al.* (1976) demonstrated that rats who were placed in a strange maze would explore it thoroughly, even if there were no rewards offered. This could be regarded as potentially life-preserving behaviour, since if a threat was presented, the rats would know which way to run for escape!

Less obvious is the motivation of the monkeys observed by Harlow *et al.* (1950). They would solve puzzles and perform difficult tasks solely for the reward of watching other monkeys through a window! As far as one can tell, there was no intrinsic benefit to the watchers; they did not learn life-saving behaviours from those whom they watched. The reason may have been to provide neural stimulation. As suggested earlier, a state of inactivity is not the brain's ideal state; monkeys in captivity may lack neural stimulation, and this may have been the motivation for their actions.

People, too, like to explore their environment, even when to do so is potentially life-threatening, as in the case of mountain-climbing or space exploration. It does not appeal to all people equally, however. According to homeostatically derived theories, if you have never climbed Everest, you should be desperate to rush off and do so! Clearly, neural stimulation is not the only motivation here. Suggestions are that certain personality traits, such as sensation seeking or a need for achievement, may influence motivation, but these do not explain why one specific activity rather than another is chosen. Curiosity and exploration have no simple explanation.

Arousal theory

Arousal has been defined as a 'state of mental readiness for activity'. Arousal is mediated in the CNS through the **reticular formation** (see Chapter 3). Low arousal may be manifest by a drowsy or bored state, indicating a low level of activity in the reticular formation and the areas of the cortex to which it projects. High arousal states, excitement, panic or hysteria, are the behavioural equivalents of high neural arousal. Arousal is nonspecific and can be assumed to apply to many forms of motivation.

Arousal theory suggests that animals, including humans, are constantly seeking an optimum level of arousal. An animal that is constantly food-seeking is unlikely to exhibit curiosity, because its arousal level is already fulfilled. Given that there is no homeostatic value in curiosity, is it simply a behaviour that occurs in a vacuum, to fill time? In humans, this is not always so; people sometimes become so involved in an activity that they forget to eat. This would seem to contradict a well-known theory of motivation proposed by Maslow (1970), that needs occur in a hierarchy; basic needs have to be satisfied first before higher, less tangible needs can be fulfilled (see Figure 5.2). This is not borne out by the fact that people will go on hunger-strike, or even die, to support a principle.

FIGURE 5.2
Maslow's hierarchy of needs

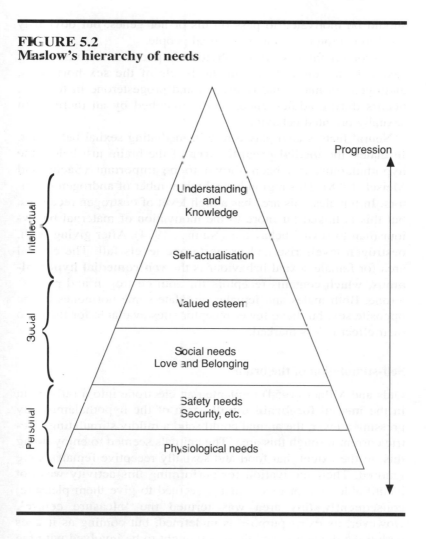

Progression

Intellectual {

Understanding
and
Knowledge

Self-actualisation

Social {

Valued esteem

Social needs
Love and Belonging

Personal {

Safety needs
Security, etc.

Physiological needs

Sexual behaviour

Whether sexual behaviour should be regarded as homeostatic or nonhomeostatic in humans is debatable. Some people lead entirely celibate lives, so sexual activity can be viewed as not essential to the maintenance of the individual, although necessary for the species. Sociobiologists would argue that the individual should be motivated to pass on his or her genes, but obviously this motivation does not apply to all people.

Hormonal factors are of obvious importance in motivating sexual behaviours. A rise in the levels of the sex hormones, androgens in males and oestrogen and progesterone in females, occurs during adolescence, and is matched by an increase in sexually oriented behaviour.

Neural factors also play a role in mediating sexual behaviour. In males, the **medial preoptic area** of the brain, just below the hypothalamus, has been shown to be important (Sachs and Meisel, 1988). This region has a high number of androgen receptors. In females, this area has a high level of oestrogen receptors, but this is linked far more to the motivation of maternal behaviour than to sexual behaviour (Numan, 1974). After giving birth, oestrogen levels rise and progesterone levels fall. The critical area for female sexual behaviour is the **ventromedial hypothalamus**, which contains receptors for both oestrogen and progesterone. Both males and females circulate some hormones of the opposite sex, but have fewer receptor sites available for them, so their effect is less marked.

Self-stimulation of the brain

Olds and Milner (1954) implanted an electrode into a rat's brain in the **medial forebrain bundle** area of the hypothalamus. By pressing a lever, the animal could send a mildly stimulating electric current through this area. The animals seemed to enjoy doing this, to the extent that food and sexually receptive females were ignored. Their motivation for performing this activity was not identifiable, except to say that it seemed to give them pleasure; consequently this area was termed the 'pleasure centre'. However, its exact purpose is undefined, but coming as it does within the dopamine circuit, it is thought to be involved with the reinforcement of activities (see Addiction, below).

Addiction

Administration of amphetamines and cocaine enhances the action of the neurotransmitter dopamine, producing an excitatory effect.

The effects of opiates and alcohol are both excitatory and inhibitory. It is thought by most researchers that the excitatory effects are those which give rise to addiction, through reinforcement by the chemical processes.

For addicts, the long-term dangers of addiction are ignored in favour of the short-term pleasure. However, in addition to the physical addiction, there is the process of psychological dependence, which is prompted by the wish to be removed from a painful situation. (A full discussion of addiction is outside the scope of this book.)

There does not seem to be a direct biochemical cause for an addiction to gambling, but it is probable that its devotees achieve a neurochemical 'high' through previous experience of winning. The irresponsible activities of some share dealers have been likened to gambling addiction, the only difference being that they are using other people's money.

Researchers have shown that genetic processes are also involved in addiction; not everyone stands an equal chance of becoming addicted to everything (Cloninger, 1987).

Consequences of addiction

Drug addiction causes a high rate of damage to the human species. Alcohol produces liver damage and cirrhosis, cerebral haemorrhage and brain damage (Korsakoff's syndrome), foetal alcohol syndrome in the babies of alcoholic mothers, and damage to innocent victims of car accidents caused through drunkenness. Cocaine and other 'illegal' drugs often cause psychosis, brain damage (especially when contaminated as 'designer drugs') and death from overdose; addicts who inject and share needles run the risk of HIV; babies may be born with brain damage and subsequent physiological and psychological problems; and a great deal of crime has been identified as emanating from the provision and acquisition of these types of drug. Smoking greatly increases the chances of lung cancer, heart disease and stroke; women who smoke often give birth to smaller babies. Those addicted to gambling run the risk of financial ruin and its associated loss of status, friends and family. The results of addiction can be far-reaching.

Summary

In this section we have looked at a wide range of motivated behaviours that are not essential to the survival of the individual. The behaviour may, in fact, be life-threatening, as in the case of many addictive behaviours. Specific neurochemical circuits have been identified as being involved in many of these motivated behaviours. While these are involved in the motivation of addiction, they do not offer a complete explanation. It is clear that psychological dependence is also involved. Nonspecific theories of motivation, such as arousal theory, attempt to explain 'why' humans should involve themselves in these activities, but no wholly satisfactory explanation has yet been offered. When this is found, society may have the answer to addiction.

Self-assessment questions

1. What is meant by nonhomeostatic motivation?
2. Describe and discuss an example of this type of motivation.
3. What does arousal theory contribute to our understanding of nonhomeostatic motivation?

SECTION III   WHAT IS EMOTION?

> Oh tell me, where is fancy bred? In the heart or in the head? How begot, how nourished?
>
> (Shakespeare, *The Merchant of Venice*, Act III, Scene 2)

By the sixteenth century, one of our greatest playwrights and a keen student of human behaviour was asking about the development, manifestation and expression of human emotions. Early philosophers who tried to represent people as rational beings came across the phenomenon of emotion, in which rationality tends to fly out of the window.

According to Darwin (1872), we should not consider ourselves the only species that has emotions. Animals, too, present fear, rage, and possibly something even akin to love: consider swans who mate for life and mourn despondently at the loss of a mate.

Darwin in fact suggested that there are specific, fundamental emotions that find expression in each individual. The exploration of the mechanisms of these emotions and their expression has kept psychologists busy for many years.

There are a number of components in emotion:

1. The perception of the emotion-arousing stimulus (*for example, an armed robber enters the bank where you are waiting*).
2. Subjective feeling or experience of emotion (pleasant/unpleasant) (*in most people, fear*).
3. Involuntary physiological changes of the body's internal balance (arousal/depression) (*arousal*).
4. External bodily changes (facial/posture) (*face shows fear, body freezes or steps back*).
5. Cognitive factors; awareness of situation, previous experience, memory (*Have seen this on television; people may get killed*).
6. Voluntary behavioural consequences; a response to the stimulus (*Do as the robber says, he has the gun!*)

While it is usually agreed that (1) comes first and (6) comes last of the above components, the order of (2) to (5), or their relative importance, is still a matter for discussion and theory, as we shall see in Section IV.

Recognising emotions

It has been suggested that we first 'name' emotions to ourselves by observing them in others. But how accurate are we in observing emotions in others? Certainly, there seem to be emotional experiences that have universally recognisable facial expressions, as crosscultural studies have shown (Morris, 1982).

Ekman (1982) suggested there are six primary emotions: sadness, happiness, fear, disgust, anger and surprise. To this list, another researcher (Plutchik, 1980) added acceptance and expectancy. Other researchers have identified 11 or more, which begs the question 'What do we mean by **primary emotions**?' Can we determine this by finding out how good we are at recognising emotions in others?

An interesting experiment was carried out by Laird (1974), which demonstrated that observers had some difficulty identifying the emotion portrayed on still photographs, although they were more accurate in identifying the posed emotion portrayed in photographs of actors. Presumably, we all have expectations of how emotions will be portrayed (which is why actors are successful here), but as humans we do not always show exactly the facial expression others would expect of us.

Feedback from facial muscles

Not only do the facial muscles expressing emotion provide feedback to the brain indicating what they are doing ('I am smiling'), but this also enhances the mood that is being experienced. This was demonstrated experimentally by Ekman (1983), who told participants he was measuring facial muscle movement and asked them to arrange their facial muscles in particular ways and hold these for ten seconds. The resulting expressions corresponded to basic emotions such as anger, disgust, happiness and fear, although the subjects were not expressly told that they were portraying emotional states.

It was found that when participants were portraying happiness and disgust, their heart rates slowed; for anger and fear, heart rates were accelerated. This would seem to suggest that feedback from facial muscles can affect autonomic arousal. In fact, these effects were stronger than when the same participants were overtly asked to 'feel' these emotions.

Neural mechanisms for the recognition of facial expressions

Facial expressions are very important to humans as a species (and other primates, too). Not only is it important for us to recognise the faces of people we know, but also their facial expressions tell us what sort of mood they are in.

Face-sensitive neurons have been identified in the **inferior cortex** of the **temporal lobe** (see Figure 5.3), in the **visual association area**, which is next to the visual cortex identified in earlier chapters. Baylis, *et al.* (1985) found that most of these neurones are sensitive to recognising differences between faces. This sensiti√i⊑y would suggest why you may well recognise someone's face but cannot remember their name!

FIGURE 5.3
Neural mechanisms for facial recognition

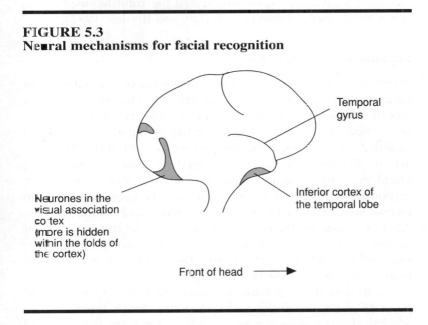

Temporal gyrus

Neurones in the
visual association
cortex
(more is hidden
within the folds of
the cortex)

Inferior cortex of
the temporal lobe

Front of head ⟶

Rolls *et al.* (1989) suggested that while this area has neurones predisposed to respond to faces, they learn to respond to a specific face and then respond differently if a new face is presented. This learning process may well be similar to that modelled by the **neural networks** that were described in Chapter 3.

However, the ability to recognise emotions in other people's faces may be mediated by a different area of the brain. Bruyer *et al.* (1983) found that a **prosopagnosic** (a person who cannot recognise faces, usually through temporal lobe damage) can still recognise and name emotions in faces. Evidence from patients with stroke or accidental brain damage suggests that the right hemisphere seems to recognise emotions more easily (Etcoff, 1985). Fried *et al.* (1982) found that stimulation of the **middle temporal gyrus** disrupted the recognition of emotions.

Recognition of emotions in others is also mediated by voice patterns, especially pitch, timing and accentuation. A rise in pitch, for example, indicates fear or alarm; this seems to be a universal signal, whereas others may be culturally based. Evidence from damaged individuals again implicated the right hemisphere as being more involved than the left (Ley and Bryden, 1982).

Physiological aspects of emotion

When we are experiencing emotion, a number of internal changes take place, which are mainly involuntary. Observation of the emotion-arousing stimulus produces activity in the cortex; subcortical structures, in particular the hypothalamus, are also 'notified'. This prompts the sympathetic section of the ANS (the activity division) into action, accelerating heart rate, increasing blood pressure, dilating pupils and all the other involuntary responses necessary for increased activity (you may wish to refresh your memory by referring to Figure 3.13, Actions of the ANS on organs of the body). The decision-making processes of the cortex decide on a suitable course of action, which is implemented by the body. Feedback from the results of this restore the body's processes to baseline (see Figure 5.4).

In addition, the hypothalamus sends nervous impulses to the pituitary gland, which brings the endocrine system into play. The adrenal glands release adrenaline, which maintains the increased heart rate, thereby assisting the body's activity. Saliva production is not needed during strong emotion, as eating and digestion will not be taking place at the same time, and insulin production and release will be slowed.

Strong emotions, such as fear, anger or extreme grief, arouse sympathetic responses in the ANS. Quieter emotions, such as contentment and sadness, are thought to activate the parasympathetic division of the ANS.

Summary

The perception of an emotion-arousing stimulus brings about physiological changes, involving the ANS and the endocrine system. Facial expressions that accompany these emotions send feedback information from the facial muscles via nerves to the cortex. Some of these facial expressions are almost certainly innate and have been demonstrated across cultures. Others may have been learned through early social interactions. The recognition of faces and facial expressions is important to us as a species in that it conveys important social information.

FIGURE 5.4
Diagrammatic representation of the physiological processes of emotion

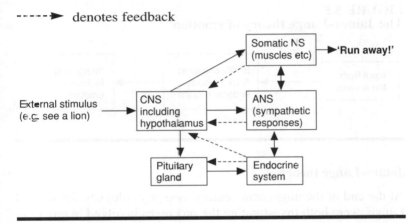

----► denotes feedback

Self-assessment questions

1. How do we recognise emotions in ourselves or others?
2. How is recognition aided by neural mechanisms?
3. What are the physiological responses associated with strong emotions?

SECTION IV THEORIES AND STUDIES OF EMOTION

At the outset of this chapter, a number of events were identified which occur during emotion. Experimental work by psychologists and physiologists has tried to identify the order of these events and what changes are associated with each event. In turn, this has given rise to a number of different theories of emotion, none of which yet seems to answer all the questions posed.

One question asks whether the **feeling** of emotion precedes or follows the **expression** of emotion. Another question is, exactly how do bodily responses vary between different emotions, or is there simply a continuum of arousal? We will look at a number of theories to see how these questions can be addressed.

FIGURE 5.5
The James–Lange theory of emotion

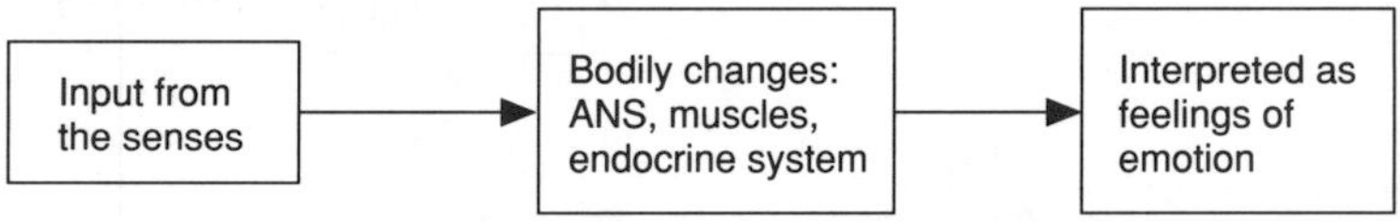

James–Lange theory

At the end of the nineteenth century, two physiologists, James and Lange, were both investigating the processes involved in emotion, although working separately. Both came to the same conclusion, which is why the theory became known as the James–Lange theory. They suggested that bodily changes produce the feelings of emotion (see Figure 5.5); you run away from the lion, which *then* promotes the feelings and recognition of fear. This seems the oppposite to the common-sense point of view.

This theory, it must be remembered, was proposed while investigations into the transmission of nerve impulses was in its infancy. James and Lange were looking at subjective experiences and trying to reconcile them with the known physiology of the time. For example, if you are crossing the road, and a car comes along unexpectedly, blowing its horn at you, you skip quickly on to the pavement. A second or so later, you realise that your heart is pounding and your knees feel shaky, yet you are now out of danger.

James and Lange were interpreting this type of phenomenon by saying that the physical action (of running out of the way) had promoted the feeling of fear (we all recognise a pounding heart and wobbly knees as the concomitants of strong emotion). With the knowledge that you now have, you will realise that the heart goes on pounding for some seconds longer because of the adrenaline released by the endocrine system, our slower-acting back-up system.

By the 1920s, physiologists such as Cannon were pointing out weaknesses in the theory:

1. People who have paralysis of the limbs and cannot take physical action still feel emotion, so the actions cannot be the cause of the feelings of emotion.
2. Sympathetic changes in the ANS are relatively slow to occur, while emotional experience is not, so physiological changes cannot be causing the feelings of an emotion.
3. Many of the same physiological changes occur in a number of different emotional states. This cannot be the only means of telling the individual which emotion is being experienced.

An interesting investigation was carried out by Hohmann (1962). Twenty-five adult males who had suffered spinal cord damage and were at least paraplegic as a result were asked about changes in emotional feelings and experiences. They reported significantly reduced emotional experiences, especially with regard to anger, fear and sexual feelings. This would seem to demonstrate that feedback from the peripheral nervous system may be necessary for the full experience of an emotion, although not as James and Lange suggested, being the primary root-cause.

Cannon–Bard theory

Cannon (1927) and a colleague, Bard, suggested a 'central' theory of emotion, called 'central' because emphasis was laid on the involvement of the central nervous system. Cannon suggested that the feeling of emotion and preparing the body for action occurred at the same time, but independently (see Figure 5.6). In addition, he proposed that the thalamus was responsible for emotional experience and the hypothalamus for the expression of emotion.

Subsequent investigations have confirmed the involvement of the hypothalamus in emotion. It sends instructions to the ANS and also the pituitary gland, which controls the endocrine system, both of which are fundamental to physiological changes during emotion. However:

- little physiological evidence has been found for the involvement of the thalamus; and
- other investigators (for example Schachter, 1964) have also questioned the likelihood of two such processes occurring at the same time but without any linkage between the two.

FIGURE 5.6
The Cannon–Bard theory of emotion

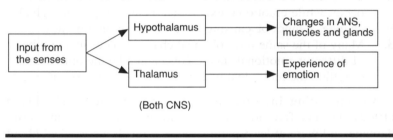

(Both CNS)

Schachter and Singer's two-factor theory

The theories we have looked at so far imply that either physiological processes determine emotional feelings or that the two occur together, but independently of each other. In 1953, **Albert Ax** tried to demonstrate a way in which the physiological processes varied for two different emotions: fear and anger. He took baseline blood levels of both adrenaline and noradrenaline, and then had his assistant play out two roles with different subjects. In the first condition, the assistant behaved in a clumsy and incompetent way, designed to produce anger in the subject, and in the second condition he set fire to the apparatus to which the subject was strapped, thereby inducing fear! (It is unlikely that this experiment would now be passed by an ethics committee!) Blood levels of adrenaline and noradrenaline were measured immediately after these two conditions, and Ax stated that fear produced higher adrenaline levels, while anger produced higher noradrenaline levels. However, subsequent researchers have been unable to replicate these results. It is unlikely that emotional differentiation could be tied to the levels of just one hormone.

Researchers realised that more than physiological factors must be involved. Schachter and Singer suggested a second factor, cognition, recognising that the observed stimulus and circumstances play a part in determining the emotion experienced.

They carried out an experiment whereby participants were injected with either adrenaline (experimental group) or a placebo (control group). (A placebo is a substance that has no demonstrable physiological effect.)

Some of the participants in the experimental group were told that they would experience autonomic arousal – increased heart and respiration rate – while the others were told that they might experience some numbness. All the participants were then placed in a room with a confederate of the experimenters, one at a time. This 'stooge' either behaved in a happy or an angry manner, to see whether the aroused participants would follow his behaviour. The participants who already had an explanation for their feelings of autonomic arousal did not follow suit; they had no need to add further cognitions to their explanation for feeling aroused. The others who had received adrenaline but no explanation, took on the happy or angry manner of the stooge. There was no change in the behaviour of the control group.

Schachter and Singer concluded from these results that, while physiological arousal is necessary in emotion, cognitive appraisal of the situation is necessary to determine the emotion associated with that arousal. Students of methodology will be interested to notice that Schachter and Singer used adrenaline as the **independent variable**, measuring reported emotional behaviour as the **dependent variable**, whereas Ax used induced emotion as the **independent variable** and measured resultant hormonal levels as the **dependent variable**.

Follow-up experiments (for example Maslach, 1979) have had some difficulty in reproducing these results and have also suggested that induced autonomic arousal produces more negative ratings than would be expected. In other words, participants stated that they were more angry than would have been expected in the 'angry stooge' situation, or less happy than would be expected in the 'happy stooge' situation. In a real-life situation, the same stimulus would elicit physiological and cognitive responses, leading the subject to **perceived** arousal and emotional feeling, which are interpreted together as the appropriate emotion.

Lazarus's cognitive theory

The importance of cognitive interpretation of circumstances in determining arousal levels is central to Lazarus's theory. He suggests that some degree of cognitive processing is essential before an emotional reaction, either overt or internal, can occur.

In an experiment (Speisman *et al.*, 1964), participants were shown a film of African tribal male circumcisions. Four different commentaries accompanied the film: Group 1 received a commentary that emphasised the pain suffered by the young boys in the film; Group 2 saw the film without any commentary; Group 3 heard a commentary that denied that much pain and suffering was involved; and Group 4 received an 'intellectual' commentary, emphasising tribal procedures and the prized entry into manhood. Emotional responses from those watching the film were highest in Group 1, followed consecutively by 2, 3 then 4. From these results, it was concluded that emotional reactions are strongly influenced by the cognition of a perceived event.

Lazarus *et al.* (1980) proposed a theory suggesting that emotion is a cognitive function, arising as a result of **appraisal** of a situation:

1. A stimulus may be appraised as **nonthreatening**, leading to positive emotional states. The actual emotion experienced depends upon other characteristics or circumstances.
2. A stimulus appraised as **threatening** leads to direct action, such as attack, retreat or freezing, together with physiological responses such as those which accompany negative states, including fear, anger or depression.
3. If direct action is impossible, **coping strategies** may be employed to reappraise the situation benignly, in order to live with the threat. These coping strategies may be simply to redefine the threat as 'not as bad as it was first perceived'.

This theory has been used to explain some forms of human behaviour, for example why a woman continues to live with a man who is violent towards her. The stimulus (the man) is appraised as threatening, but for various reasons the woman cannot take direct action. She cannot fight back, he is stronger; she cannot run away, she has nowhere to go. The solution is to reappraise the situation.

Perhaps he won't hit me again, he is very contrite next day, and so on. Living with this reappraised threat is less problematic than fear of the unknown life outside of that situation.

This theory is primarily descriptive, but the underlying mechanisms involved in emotion, the relationship between cognitions, feelings and expressions of emotion, are largely undefined.

Arousal theory and emotion

A number of researchers have suggested that arousal theory could form the basis of a theory of emotion, given that arousal is a nonspecific physiological response, heightening a person's awareness. Mandler (1982), for example, suggested that the interruption of ongoing thought processes or behaviour sequences is sufficient to activate the ANS. This creates a state of general physiological arousal, which is then given an emotional label, based on a cognitive interpretation of the situation or stimulus. This would seem to suggest that all emotional physiological responses are the same and that differentiation arises solely at cognitive level. However, sadness and depression are seen as parasympathetic responses and not simply a lack of arousal.

Social theories of emotion

There are a number of theories of emotion that concentrate either wholly or primarily on the social aspect of emotion. As this book is mainly concerned with the relationship between psychological and physiological phenomena, these will be mentioned only briefly.

Averill's social theory.

Averill sees emotions as **transitory social roles**: a person adopts the role defined by his or her culture for the emotion being experienced.

Weiner's attributional theory

Attribution theory suggests that we attribute causes to all events that happen, whether or not we have adequate information to do so. Weiner (1985) sees emotions as coming from these attributions. These may initially be just 'good' or 'bad' reactions, which are then refined into recognisable emotions once a cause has been attributed to the situation.

Summary

A wide range of theories has been offered concerning emotional states, none of which has wholly explained the relationship between our physiological responses, our cognitions and our feelings of emotion. That there is a relationship has been demonstrated by a number of studies, but whether the factors are sequential or concurrent, whether one has more importance than the others, is not clear as yet.

Self-assessment questions

1. Which physiological mechanisms are involved in emotions?
2. Explain, quoting experimental evidence, why cognitive factors need to be involved in any explanation of emotion.
3. Describe **one** theory of emotion that is supported by experimental evidence, including a brief description of this evidence.

SECTION V   MOTIVATION, AGGRESSION AND EMOTION

What causes aggression? Does it occur because of the frustration of our wants, needs and desires? Is it due to finding ourselves in a situation in which we feel we cannot cope and that the only route is to strike out? Is it a result of faulty learning processes, possibly instilled at an early age, where the only way 'to be' in a tough world is to be the aggressor rather than the aggressed? Perhaps physiological processes cause us to be aggressive. Or is it simply that all people are innately aggressive, but some more so than others, just as some people have darker hair or bluer eyes. Instead of philosophising, we will examine what is known about aggression.

The frustration–aggression hypothesis

This suggests that aggression stems from the frustration of plans or needs, and was originally suggested by Dollard *et al.* (1939). Frustration creates a state of autonomic arousal, which results in aggression as an outlet, because the desired activity is being thwarted. This does not explain why everyone who experiences frustration does not resort to aggression. Neither does it explain why aggression should result, rather than any other demonstration of high autonomic arousal.

Aggressive instincts

According to the ethologist Konrad Lorenz (1966), animals have instinctive aggression that they use in order to fight for food, territory and mates, and to protect their young. He also suggested that fighting between members of a species stops short before actual killing takes place, humans being the only exception. This, he suggested, was due to the fact that, in the natural state, people lacked natural weapons, such as large canine teeth or horns, with which to kill opponents, so the mechanism inhibiting the use of these was also lacking.

Subsequent studies have shown that this is not so (see Malim *et al.* 1996, for a fuller account of this). Chimpanzees, close to *Homo sapiens* on the phylogenetic scale, have been observed to carry out a form of gang warfare (Goodall, 1978), females behaving equally aggressively, although with less deadly effect, as their teeth are not as large or sharp (Smuts *et al.*, 1987). Wilson (1983) suggests that there are more murders among animal species than there are among humans, even taking our wars into account.

Investigators have suggested that there are three types of aggression shown by animals: defensive, offensive and predatory. Those of us in urbanised societies no longer have to hunt for our food; our capacity for predatory aggression (if it exists) may be utilised in other ways. Defensive and offensive aggression can be recognised in humans without great difficulty.

If humans, like other animals, have a natural propensity for aggression, what is the mechanism for implementing and controlling this? It would be a neat solution to identify an 'aggression centre' in the brain, but this does not appear to exist.

Neural mechanisms involved in aggression

Certain subcortical areas of the brain have been demonstrated to be involved in aggression in animals, but whether this information can be generalised to humans is less clear.

Two areas of the **midbrain** have been shown to be involved in organising aggressive behaviour, for both offensive and defensive behaviours (Adams, 1986; Depaulis *et al.*, 1989). The **hypothalamus** appears to control the occurrence and frequency of aggressive behaviours but does not directly control the behaviours (Adams, 1979). In animals, the **amygdala** modulates aggressive behaviours; it also inhibits aggression towards an individual who has previously inflicted defeat. Oestrogen and androgen receptors are present in the amygdala; their role in aggression will be examined next.

Hormones and aggression

Many years ago, Beeman (1947) found that castration of male rats reduced aggression, and injections of testosterone temporarily reinstated it. The male hormone was strongly implicated, and further studies confirmed this. Conner and Levine (1969) found that male rats who had high testosterone levels at birth needed smaller injections of testosterone in adulthood to promote aggressive behaviour than did others, although the preinjection levels of both adult groups had been similar. Neural circuits that control aggression appear to be prompted by hormonal levels, possibly through receptors in the amygdala.

Females also circulate some male hormones, just as males circulate female hormones, but at much lower levels than their opposite sex. This would seem to be the obvious explanation for aggression being viewed as more prevalent among males. A female foetus next to a male foetus in the uterus will receive prenatal androgenisation (in other words, a dose of male hormone), but this is unlikely to affect male/female behaviours after birth.

Are female hormones implicated in aggressive acts? In women, researchers have found lowest levels of aggression around the time of ovulation, when oestradiol levels are high, and highest aggression levels coincide with high progesterone immediately preceding menstruation. In animals other than humans, maternal aggression (defence of young) is a well-recognised occurrence. Women, too, exhibit fiercely protective behaviour if they feel their young are threatened. In animals, the triggers for maternal behaviour are usually sensory – the sight, smell or sound of the young; in women, the mechanisms of maternal defensive aggression have not been clearly identified.

Social and environmental factors

It is beyond the scope of this book to investigate fully the role played by social and environmental factors, in both the learning and the production of aggressive behaviour in humans. Many social and social learning studies have shown the importance of reinforcement and imitation in producing aggressive behaviour. For example, Bandura *et al.* (1963) allowed children to watch an adult behaving aggressively towards a doll. The child subsequently produced the same aggressive behaviours modelled by the adult.

It has been suggested that some environments, such as those that are overcrowded, produce aggression in the inhabitants. This was demonstrated experimentally with rats (Calhoun, 1962). Rats who lived in overcrowded conditions behaved more aggressively, including displaying infanticide, than did litter mates who were not overcrowded. It would not be possible to reproduce this experiment with humans, for ethical reasons. In the real-life situation other factors in addition to overcrowded conditions are likely to affect levels of aggression.

SUMMARY

Hormonal influences, especially of the male hormone, testosterone, are recognised by neural circuits shown to be involved in aggression. These mechanisms are present from birth but vary in sensitivity between individuals. Control of these mechanisms may be influenced by social learning and environmental circumstances, particularly in humans.

The motivation of aggression may well be homeostatic, striving for food or territory. In urbanised societies, this is less likely, and motivations may well be emotionally based, owing to frustration or anger, dislike of others or disempowerment due to one's circumstances. Strong emotions activate the ANS and hormonal systems, which provide fuel for the mechanisms of aggression.

Social and environmental factors undoubtedly play a large – if not a major – role in human aggression. Our physiology may have provided the mechanisms and our advanced brains the ingenuity for the process of aggression, but our societies provide the environment and the encouragement for its implementation.

SELF-ASSESSMENT QUESTIONS

1. What are the arguments for and against the suggestion that aggression is innate?
2. What neural and hormonal mechanisms are involved in aggression?
3. In humans, why are social and environmental factors important?

FURTHER READING

K. J. Lorenz, *On Aggression* (London: Methuen, 1966).

T. Malim, A. Birch and S. Hayward, *Comparative Psychology: A sociobiological approach* (Basingstoke: Macmillan, 1996).

Is this guy real? Fancy asking students if they know what stress is!

Stress and Anxiety 6

By the end of this chapter you will be able to:

- discuss what may cause stress;
- describe physiological responses to stress;
- outline a number of models of stress;
- identify variables involved with individual experiences of stress; and
- discuss ways of coping with stress and managing stress.

INTRODUCTION

Anxiety is an emotion that is distressing. Sometimes, it may have no specific cause, unlike fear, the cause of which can be seen and dealt with by fighting or running away. Anxiety produces the same physiological response as fear – an increase in sympathetic activity in the ANS – but this level may be maintained for some time if the individual cannot find a way of removing the source of anxiety.

This feeling of anxiety is frequently generalised from one situation or stimulus to another; Freud referred to this as 'free-floating anxiety'. If the individual does not relate the feeling of anxiety to one specific cause, it becomes extremely difficult to resolve satisfactorily.

Russell Davies (1987) suggests that anxiety states are often learned by classical conditioning (see Birch and Hayward, 1994).

An anxiety-producing situation occurs at the same time as another stimulus (for example, a child may learn that pain is associated with a doctor), so that whenever the stimulus-object appears, anxiety is aroused. In the case of our example, the doctor is not the cause of the pain but the association has been made; each time the doctor appears, anxiety is renewed, even though the pain may be absent.

Avoidance of the stimulus is a method that individuals often use to reduce anxiety. However, this means that the real source of anxiety is never explored and conquered. Sufferers of social phobia (fear of social situations) or agoraphobia (fear of open spaces) avoid the anxiety-producing situations and convince themselves that life is normal, that they have no problems. When there is no escape from an anxiety-provoking situation, **learned helplessness** may be the response. This was identified by Seligman (1975); when a noxious stimulus or event is repeatedly presented, and there is no escape route available, the individual simply accepts all that is coming and goes on with his or her life after it has passed – until the next time. This learned helplessness can be generalised from one situation to another, until the individual feels that he or she has little, if any, control over life events. This usually results in a state of depression.

Prolonged anxiety or depression can lead a state of stress, which is a recognisable physiological condition, with psychological causes and outcomes of impaired physical and psychological abilities.

What is stress?

If you asked a number of people this question, you would be given a variety of responses. Some would interpret the word 'stress' as relating to stressful situations, others would describe how they feel when stressed, and still others would describe how they dealt with stress.

The **stressor** is the situation, individual or object that causes a state of stress in the individual or an internal state of conflict that will cause stress. Stressors are not necessarily the same for all people; what appears stressful to one is merely a challenge, or all-in-a-day's-work for someone else.

FIGURE 6.1
Stressors lead to stress responses

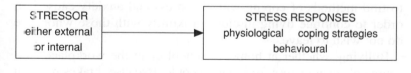

Stress responses or stress results are:

- **physiological**, in that the body makes changes in order to respond to the stress state;
- **behavioural** – the individual may change behaviour in order to deal with the stress; and
- **coping strategies**, which may or may not involve a change of overt behaviour (described in Section IV).

Anxiety and stress may produce anger and aggression in some people, apathy and depression in others. So far, research has not positively identified why individuals of the same species may produce opposite responses to the same stimulus; differences may be due partly to personality, and partly to environmental variables.

SECTION I   STRESSORS

What causes you stress? The following may be factors:

- *People*. Stress may be the result of conflict with parents, children, lovers or others with whom we come into conflict.
- *Situations*. For instance jobs, driving or internal conflicts resulting from situations in which we find ourselves.
- *Environmental events*. Noise or high temperatures, for example.

We would all undoubtedly produce a different list. Some stressors can be removed at source, others, for a variety of reasons, cannot and therefore have to be tolerated.

Other people

Frequently, the people who cause us stress are those we care about the most, and we would not want them 'removed'. We have to find methods of coping with the stress and anxiety caused, in order to continue living in close proximity with those whom we do not wish to leave.

Bullying, whether at home, at school or in the workplace, is a source of severe stress from other people. Because it takes place in a 'closed' situation, usually without any moral or physical support for the victims, the 'flight' route is not open to them. Through physical or psychological weaknesses, the victim is precluded from the 'fight' response as well, and tends to try to avoid the bullies, by staying away from work or school, with long-term detrimental effects for the victim. Victims feel that they cannot tell others of their problem, for a variety of reasons. For example, they may believe they will be subjected to even greater abuse, or others will simply laugh and tell them to 'stand up for yourself'. (If they could do so, they would not be bullied in the first place.) Or they may be denying, even to themselves, that the problem exists, that the abuse is intended as fun. Various coping strategies are employed, most of which are ineffective. Usually, the victim needs outside help in order to resolve the problem permanently (Adams, 1992).

Bullying at home, whether it is abuse of a spouse or children, is an even more serious problem, because the victim can see no retreat from the situation. Women's refuges and children's helplines have been set up as initial responses. A full discussion of this problem is beyond the scope of this book.

Internal conflicts

Internal conflicts arise when an individual has to decide between two incompatible or mutually exclusive choices. These may be alternatives that are equally attractive, called **approach/approach conflicts** (Shall I join the hockey team or the netball team? I don't have time to do both), or equally unattractive, called **avoidance/avoidance conflicts** (you don't want to take this dead-end job, but you don't want to starve).

Sometimes, the action you might wish to take has penalties attached (**approach/avoidance conflicts**), and you have to decide whether these are worth suffering (I would like to apply for a psychology degree, but I don't want to do the statistics necessary). Resolving inner conflicts can be very stressful; usually, the problems and alternatives are more serious than those suggested above.

Erikson (1980) in his theory of development, suggested some conflicts that arise when our inner motives are in opposition:

- *Autonomy versus dependence.* We experience a desire to be independent, but it also feels safer to be dependent on someone we view as stronger than ourselves.
- *Intimacy versus isolation.* We wish to be close to another, to share innermost thoughts and feelings, but fear we may be betrayed.
- *Co-operation versus competition.* From childhood onwards, competition is encouraged in individuals, but they are also urged to co-operate and help others. Both at school and at work, this presents problems of deciding which course of action to take in which set of circumstances, and there are social penalties for making the wrong choice.

There are also cultural norms of behaviour and morality, which we are expected to observe. These often run contrary to our basic instincts: to fight or run away. A soldier may experience such fear that he would prefer to run, but society expects him to fight. A woman may want to thrash her husband's lover, but this would be condemned by many societies. Inner conflicts produced by blocking these actions lead to stress.

Life changes and daily hassles

Events that happen in our lives can also produce stress. Holmes and Rahe (1967) investigated the relative strengths of a number of these life events and produced a rating scale (The Social Readjustment Rating Scale, see Figure 6.2), equating numerical values with a range of life events, from the most severe (death of a spouse) to lesser events, such as a change in eating habits. You may not rank these in the same order, but, on the whole, consensus is high (Holmes and Masuda, 1974).

FIGURE 6.2
Social readjustment rating scale

Rank	Life event	Mean value
1	Death of a spouse	100
2	Divorce	73
3	Marital separation	65
4	Jail term	63
5	Death of close family member	63
6	Personal injury or illness	53
7	Marriage	50
8	Fired at work	47
9	Marital reconciliation	45
10	Retirement	45
11	Change in health of family member	44
12	Pregnancy	40
13	Sex difficulties	39
14	Gain of new family member	39
15	Business readjustment	39
16	Change in financial state	38
17	Death of close friend	37
18	Change to different line of work	36
19	Change in number of arguments with spouse	35
20	Mortgage over £60 000	31
21	Foreclosure of mortgage or loan	30
22	Change in responsibilities at work	29
23	Son or daughter leaving home	29
24	Trouble with in-laws	29
25	Outstanding personal achievement	28
26	Wife begins or stops work	26
27	Begin or end school	26
28	Change in living conditions	25
29	Revision of personal habits	24
30	Trouble with boss	23
31	Change in work hours or conditions	20
32	Change in residence	20
33	Change in schools	20
34	Change in recreation	19
35	Change in church activities	19
36	Change in social activities	18
37	Mortgage or loan less than £10 000	17
38	Change in sleeping habits	16
39	Change in number of family get-togethers	15
40	Change in eating habits	15
41	Vacation	13
42	Christmas	12
43	Minor violation of the law	11

Source: Adapted from Holmes and Rahe (1967)

To calculate the amount of stress experienced by an individual, over a given period of time (usually between six months and two years), the rank value of all that person's reported life events is totalled. This gives a Life Change Score, which can be examined in conjunction with the individual's physical and mental well-being. Investigators have found that a high Life Change Score is often followed by physical illness or psychological problems a year or two later (Rahe and Arthur, 1977). Presumably, the stress induced by life changes lowers the functioning of the immune system, causing illnesses to be contracted more easily.

Critics of the life events scale point out that it is difficult to separate other variables, which may be causes of the ill-health, from the apparent effects of life changes. For example, death of a wife may cause a man to change his lifestyle, to adopt an unhealthy diet, to drink and smoke more; it may be these variables that actually produce the breakdown in health.

Other critics suggest that the gradual breakdown in health may be the cause rather than the effect of the life events. Poor health may induce absenteeism or inefficiency at work, which may result in the loss of a job. There is also a 'correlational effect' attached to mental ill-health: depressed people tend to report more negative events. It is difficult to say whether the depression or the reporting of the events is the cause or the effect. In addition, the scale does not allow for the fact that people's circumstances vary widely. What may be a traumatic event for one person may be a release for another; for example, individuals' responses to divorce vary widely.

Lazarus (1966) suggested that **daily hassles** cause more stress problems than do life events. Small daily problems can summate until we feel we cannot cope. DeLongis *et al.* (1982) found that daily hassles were a better predictor of ill-health than were life events. Lazarus also suggested that the effects of hassles were offset by 'uplifts' – good events that happened in our day. These were balanced by the individual, providing an overall 'feel' to the day, and changing the individual's perception of feeling stressed.

Traumatic events

Situations outside the normal range of human experience are recognised as being highly stressful. These include earthquakes, floods, serious car, train or plane accidents, wars, or witnessing or being a victim of violent crimes, such as rape, assault or murder. Many survivors experience **post-traumatic stress disorder**, which may develop immediately after the disaster or some time later. Initially, sufferers may feel numb to the world, then may repeatedly relive the experience in 'flashbacks' or dreams. They may exhibit anxiety, depression or overalertness, and sometimes feelings of guilt that they have survived while others perished.

Job stress

Stress at work may be due to a number of causes, some due to unpleasant physical environments (noisy or polluted) or incompatibility with other workers. French *et al.* (1982) suggested it is often attributable to a poor **person–environment fit**. This implies more than just the physical workspace, and involves a problem with the job itself, feeling like a square peg in a round hole. This produces stress in the person, who feels that he or she should change in order to do the job better but is unable to see how this can be accomplished. Inflexible work practices mean that the job task itself cannot be changed, so the result is impasse and greater stress.

Job strain is often produced by having too much – or too little – to do, or by having too difficult or too easy a job.

Frustration at work, by not being able to achieve what the individual would like to achieve, through lack of facilities or other circumstances, produces stress and may lead to **burnout**. This is a feeling of mental and physical exhaustion, a sense of futility and ultimately a lack of care for others (Maslach and Jackson, 1981). This syndrome has been reported among nurses and other care-workers, who feel depersonalised by their workload, compared with the resources they have available (for example Jackson *et al.*, 1986).

Other environmental stressors

Noise, pollution and extremes of heat or cold may account for feelings of stress. These are all subject to a wide variety of mitigating circumstances, and there is a great deal of difference between individual responses to these stressors. By and large, the factors that best predict how stressful these are seen to be are **predictability** and **controllability**.

Predictability

If we can predict when an event is likely to occur, it is perceived as being less stressful (Katz and Wykes, 1985). We find it very difficult to cope with uncertainty. Hunter (1979) found that women whose husbands were reported missing in action in the Vietnam War, reported poorer health than those who knew they had been widowed; the uncertainty was more stressful than widowhood.

Controllability

Similarly, feeling that one has control over the events in one's life makes those events seem less stressful. Over the past ten years, surveys have been carried out with more than 20000 civil servants. Questions were asked concerning health-related behaviours, such as smoking and drinking, and work-related questions, such as perceived sources of pressure at work. Physiological measures were also taken, for example ECGs (to detect heart problems) and blood samples, to measure levels of, among other things, cholesterol. High levels of cholesterol have long been associated with coronary heart disease (CHD), so this was to serve as an indicator of those at risk.

It was found that there was a strong relationship between high cholesterol levels and grades of employment, but not in the direction that might be expected. The highest cholesterol levels were found among the lowest grades of civil servants, and a gradation showed until the lowest cholesterol levels were shown among the highest grades of civil servants. The lower the grade, the less control the individual has over work conditions and decision making processes. It could be concluded that lack of control may have been causing stress, which related to increased cholesterol levels and the risk of heart disease (Brunner *et al.*, 1993).

Lack of control seems to be a feature in a number of people's lives, and, rather than whether they eat a great deal of fish and chips (as suggested by a recently-deposed health official!), may be the cause of stress, high cholesterol and heart attacks, although diet may be a contributory factor.

SECTION II   MODELS OF STRESS

A number of models of stress have been produced to explain and describe what happens to an individual in a stress state. We will examine some of these, commencing with a physiological model, which explains the body's responses to stress, but does not differentiate responses to specific stressors. We will then examine some interactional models, which look at the processes involved between stressor and stressed.

Physiological Model

Physiological changes in response to stress are similar, although not identical, in all individuals. These changes were identified by Selye (1956), who called them the **general adaptation syndrome**. He identified three stages of response (see Figure 6.3).

Stage 1: Alarm

The body's 'fight or flight' responses are activated against the perceived threat. The hypothalamus sends impulses to the sympathetic division of the ANS, which increases heart rate, respiration rate and blood pressure, dilates pupils, releases glycogen, and brings about GSR (galvanic skin response: the electrical conductivity of the skin) changes through sweating. The hypothalamus also prompts the endocrine system, via the pituitary, which releases ACTH (adrenocorticotrophic hormone). This travels to the adrenal glands, which release adrenaline and noradrenaline, thus perpetuating the responses implemented by the sympathetic division of the ANS. The corticosteroids (cortisone and hydrocortisol) are also released from the adrenals. These are also involved in the stress response, maintaining the body's responses.

Stage 2: Resistance

If the stressor is not removed, some of the immediate responses decrease in intensity. Sympathetic activity declines but maintains a level of constant readiness. Adrenaline levels remain high, however; the physical activity of fighting or running away has not been consummated, although the individual may perform other actions that are ineffective. High adrenaline levels are instrumental in depressing the body's immune responses. The immune system is responsible for warding off attack from external sources.

FIGURE 6.3
The general adaptation syndrome

When a stressor occurs, the body's resistance initially drops, then rises sharply. It stays high throughout the second stage of the response, but ultimately can be sustained no longer and falls in exhaustion. If a second stressor is added to the first (see lower dotted curve), resistance is lower throughout and exhaustion reached sooner.

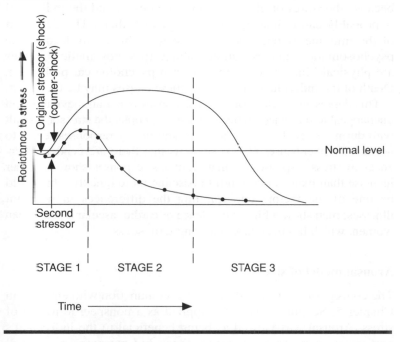

Chronic (long-term) stress leads to a depletion of the body's resources and a reduction in the effectiveness of the immune system. The number of white blood cells (lymphocytes), which are essential to the immune system, is reduced under stress. Schleifer *et al.* (1979) reported that men whose wives had died from breast cancer showed depleted counts of lymphocytes within a month of the spouse's death, these remaining low for the following year.

Health problems that have been indicated as resulting from or being linked with stress include cancer, heart attacks, ulcers, colitis, asthma, hypertension (high blood pressure) and rheumatoid arthritis. In addition, depletion of the immune system leaves the body susceptible to attack by bacteria and viruses, causing a variety of minor illnesses.

Stage 3: Exhaustion.

The body's resources are depleted; blood glucose levels drop because the stores of glycogen have been used, and the individual is probably eating inadequately to replenish them. The depletion of the immune system results in disease, which may lead to the psychosomatic illnesses outlined above (psychosomatic illnesses are physical illnesses that are rooted in psychological problems). Death of the individual from one of these causes may be the result.

This depressing picture of stress responses is not an inevitable and unchangeable sequence. In the majority of people, the stressor is dealt with during Stage 1 or early Stage 2, and bodily responses return to normal. Frankenhauser (1983) suggests that there are gender differences in stress responses, in that women's responses show a higher increase than males', but return to baseline more quickly. This could be one of the factors underpinning the differences in resultant illnesses; men show a higher incidence of cardiovascular disease than women, which has been linked to long-term stress.

Arousal model of stress

The concept of arousal as described in conjunction with emotion in Chapter 5, Section 4, was also applied as a nonspecific model of stress. Arousal was viewed as being beneficial to the individual's performance, up to an optimum level, but extremes of arousal produced stress and a corresponding decrement in performance (Yerkes-Doson Law, see Figure 6.4). You may have noticed this phenomenon yourself: if you become too highly stressed before an exam, perhaps because you are desperate to do well, your performance is likely to be lower than you would expect of yourself.

The nonspecific idea of arousal would suggest that all stimuli would produce the same pattern of arousal; in real life, researchers have not found this to be so. As a model of stress, the concept of arousal has limited use.

FIGURE 6.4
The relationship between arousal and performance

Performance increases up to an optimum level of arousal; if arousal continues to increase, performance declines. Stress may occur. A higher level of arousal is necessary for a simple, boring task while a slightly lower level of arousal is better for a more complex task. Arousal levels vary between individuals.

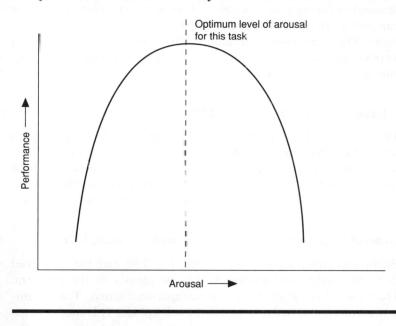

Psychosocial stimuli model

Kagan and Levi (1975) suggested that psychosocial stimuli, such as life changes, prepare an individual for coping with stress.

The extent to which they do so is influenced by genetic differences and learning experiences, which are subsequently reflected in the physiological stress response identified by Seyle. However, even the authors admitted that this is a simple model; many facets began to be recognised as being implicated in stress.

Person–environment transaction model (Cox and Mackay, 1976)

Cox and Mackay suggested that stress is due to a dynamic transaction between the individual and the environment (see Figure 6.5). Important to this model is the individual's cognitive assessment of the perceived demands made on him or her, and that individual's perceived capability to deal with those demands. Stress is the result of the perceived demand outweighing the perceived capability. For example, an individual may perceive that the demand of taking four A-levels in two years outweighs his or her capability. If the individual is pressured to do so, stress may result. This perception is influenced by a number of factors, such as personality, situational demands, previous experiences and any current stress state already existing.

Interactional model (Lazarus, 1976)

The view of stress proposed by Lazarus (1976) included the suggestion that the individual's perception of capability interacted with cognitive appraisal of the threat. Again, a mismatch of the two resulted in stress. Lazarus also looked at the role of frustration and conflict within the individual, in exacerbating stress.

General facet model of stress (Beehr and Newman, 1978)

Beehr and Newman identified more than 150 variables involved in stress, giving recognition to the complexity of the problem. Their model is largely based on occupational stress. The organisation referred to in the model is the workplace. This model gives recognition to changes occurring over time and feedback to the individual, which then results in personality and other changes. This is important in that subsequent reactions to stress may be influenced by these changes.

FIGURE 6.5
Transactional model of stress

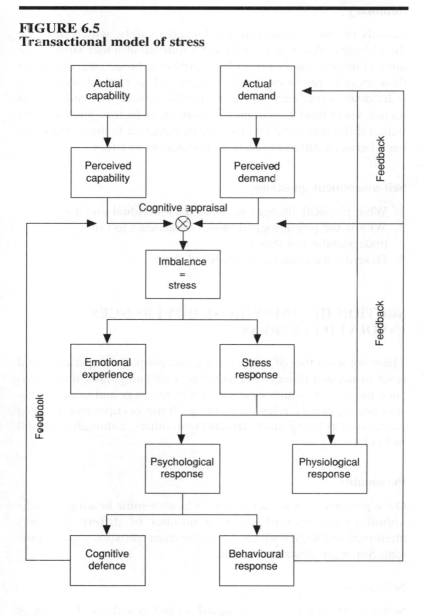

Source: T. Cox, Stress, *Macmillan Press, 1978*

Summary

Models of stress include physiological models, which describe the changes taking place within the individual under stress. The arousal model is only useful for identifying broad patterns rather than specific reactions. Early models fail to explain why some individuals experience stress in specific situations, while others do not. Later models take into account other factors, such as individual differences and localised environmental factors, and feedback between different facets and responses to stress.

Self-assessment questions

1. What physical changes occur in the individual under stress?
2. Why is the physiological model inadequate to our understanding of stress?
3. Describe a transactional model of stress.

SECTION III   INDIVIDUAL DIFFERENCES INVOLVED IN STRESS

There are a number of factors that cause people to experience and react to stress differently. Personality, race and gender may influence the way in which a person reacts to stress and which stressors are especially relevant to them. Some occupations are also recognised as being more stressful than others, although not to all individuals equally.

Personality

Once personality was recognised as having some bearing on individual experiences of stress, a number of different studies attempted to identify which particular characteristics were important. Some are described below.

Self-esteem

Self-esteem is the level of regard an individual has for him or herself. Extremely high levels of self-esteem may mean that the individual is over-confident and possibly unrealistic in expectations of self-efficacy. **Self-efficacy** is an individual's belief that he or she can perform required tasks and behaviours effectively. Low levels of self-esteem may indicate feelings of worthlessness, possibly resulting in depression and anxiety. A moderately high level of self-esteem has been shown to be associated with good mental health (Coopersmith 1968).

Locus of control

This concept was suggested by Rotter (1966) to identify how people saw the relationship between events and themselves. Each person has a locus of control that is either primarily **external** or primarily **internal**. We see our lives as being controlled by events outside the self if we have an external locus of control, or as being under the control of the self if we have an internal locus of control.

People with either an internal or an external locus of control can be subject to stress. Those who see themselves as recipients of all that life throws at them can come to view life as malevolent or depressing (this can be a precursor to Seligman's concept of 'learned helplessness'). Those who have an internal locus of control not only see themselves as being in control of their lives, but are also prone to blame themselves for things that go wrong. During a 'bad spell' (which we all have sometimes!) this self-blame can prove stressful. However, Johnson and Sarason (1978) found a higher incidence of depression and anxiety among those rated as high on external locus of control.

Type A/Type B

Type A behaviour was the phrase coined by Friedman and Rosenman (1974) to describe certain behaviour patterns displayed by patients who had developed coronary heart disease. Studies indicated that men who exhibited these patterns were two and a half times more likely to develop heart disease than were men who did not show these behaviours (Type B).

Type A behaviours include being ambitious, competitive, alert, impatient and aggressive. Their speech is hurried, they gesture frequently and they have difficulty letting others finish what they want to say before interrupting. They are always in a hurry, to the point of appearing 'driven', showing chronically high levels of arousal. They exhibit 'deadline urgency' (having to get things done by a certain time) and extreme competitiveness, even in leisure pursuits. (See Figure 6.6).

FIGURE 6.6
Are you a Type A?

FUN QUIZ

1. If you find you have 10 minutes to spare, do you:
   (a) squeeze in another job, or
   (b) have a cup of tea?

2. If you see someone struggling with a new task, do you:
   (a) take the job and do it yourself, or
   (b) just watch and encourage them?

3. If you are playing a game with a friend and you lose, do you:
   (a) feel angry with yourself,
   (b) shrug and go for a Coke?

4. When you finish a meal, do you:
   (a) get up and get going on the next job, or
   (b) sit at the table and chat?

SCORE

Three or four (a)s – take the heat off yourself, or life may be too short to worry!

Two (a)s – take life as it comes. **No (a)s** – life could just pass you by!

Type B personalities may be equally ambitious, but do not appear 'driven'. Their job ambitions do not dominate their entire lives. They find time for family and friends, and tend to choose leisure pusuits that are less competitive than the Type A's choice.

Type A men are often highly successful in their jobs, so their activities are not discouraged at work. Ganster (1986) suggested that Type A behaviour may promote the risk of cardiac disease because it involves that system in the stress respose. Organisations should weigh this risk against the desire for high performance from its Type A employees.

Other studies have found that the Type A personality appears to be involved in cardiovascular disease but is not a reliable predictor for this (Matthews, 1988).

These studies have all looked at men's responses, partly because at the time they were conducted, there were fewer women in executive and managerial positions and fewer women exhibiting cardivascular disease. Currently, the incidence of both of these has risen, although women still lag behind on the managerial and heart disease fronts. The rises may not be directly correlated because there are other confounding variables. For example, more women have taken up smoking, which is a known causal factor in cardiovascular problem. Women may be resistant to 'executive stress', but if they smoke, it could be this which is causing the rise in heart disease, which may be wrongly correlated with stress.

'Hardy' personality

Some individuals seem to cope well with one stressful event after another, while others break down under very little pressure. Researchers have attempted to verify why this should be so; personality characteristics is one area of study.

Kobasa (1979) gave questionnaires to 600 executives or managers, asking them to itemise illnesses and stressful events they had experienced in the previous three years. Personality questionnaires were also completed. From the responses, Kobasa analysed two groups of responses. Both groups had scored above average on stressful events, but one group scored below average on illnesses, while the other group scored above average.

From the analysis it was found that the group of high stress/low illness group:

- felt more in control of their lives;
- were more actively involved in their work and social lives; and
- were more oriented towards challenges and change.

Critics of this study suggested that these characteristics could be the result, rather than the cause, of illnesses; for example, it is hard to become totally absorbed in your work or social life if you are ill. Subsequently, a longitudinal study (Kobasa *et al.*, 1982) monitored executives for two years and identified that those who set out with positive attitudes were the ones who suffered fewest illnesses.

The personality characterisitics of these **hardy** individuals include **control**, **commitment** and **challenge**. Control, as we have discussed earlier, has been demonstrated as a buffer to stress. Commitment may typify those with firm social support systems around them, while challenge involves cognitive appraisal of situations in order to reassess them benignly.

However, is this type of personality available to everyone? If you have a low-interest job, you probably feel little commitment to it; it provides you with little challenge, and you almost certainly have no control over your area of work. You may argue that the essential characteristics could be assembled into interests outside work, but a 40-hour week at a boring job leaves people feeling stressed and therefore too tired to undertake challenging outside interests. It must be remembered that Kobasa's work was undertaken with executives and managers, who do not have exclusive rights to feeling stressed.

Occupations

It is implicit that some occupations are more stressful than others: doctors and other caring professionals frequently suffer from high stress levels, with nurses top of the list (Wolfgang, 1988). Other professions, which may appear to be open to dangerous situations, such as the police, have been demonstrated to suffer much lower levels of stress than expected (Jermier *et al.*, 1989), reported stress emanating from overload of paperwork rather than fear of danger on the streets! Occupational stress undoubtedly needs to be assessed to give an overall comprehensive picture of stress.

Gender

Many facets of stress and stress responses show male/female differences. For example, while Type A behaviour may not be exclusive to males, the associated correlation with cardiovascular disease is much stronger in males than females. Frankenhauser (1983) reported sex differences in the physiological responses to stressors; females showed a much sharper rise in sympathetic responses, but returned to baseline more quickly.

There are also still differences in the ratio of males to females in a number of occupations; the resultant differences in stress levels may reflect these job differences.

Surveys have shown that, where both partners in a marriage or a household have full-time jobs, the female still takes more responsibility for the home making and child rearing. This would appear to suggest greater stress on the female partner, trying to do 'two jobs'. Studies have demonstrated that women with children and full-time jobs show more instances of ill-health than do those without children.

Women often have stronger social support systems in place in their lives, which may mitigate the levels of stress experienced; this is discussed futher in the next section.

Summary

Many factors influence the things we find stressful as individuals and the way in which we respond. Personality variables, both types (such as the 'hardy' personality) and traits (such as self-esteem), gender, race and occupation all have bearing on the way we encounter stressors and the way in which we deal with them.

Self-assessment questions

1. Describe a personality trait and say why it may produce stress in an individual.
2. Describe (a) a personality type likely to experience stress, and (b) a personality type resistant to stress.
3. How does either race or gender influence the experience of stress?
4. Discuss whether occupation has any bearing on stress in the individual.

SECTION IV   COPING WITH STRESS

Anxiety and stress are disturbing experiences, producing high levels of physiological arousal, which motivates the individual to try to reduce the stress level; this process is called 'coping'. Some

coping processes will be briefly described here; they are relevant to a book on physiological psychology in that they are instrumental in reducing autonomic arousal and thereby returning physiological processes to baseline, but a full discussion of their application is outside the scope of this volume.

Lazarus & Folkman (1984) suggest there are two main forms of coping: **emotion-focused coping** and **problem-focused coping**.

Emotion-focused coping

Social support

At home   Social support processes are the network of friends and relatives willing to provide psychological assistance, even if only a willing ear, in times of stress. A number of studies have shown that where social support networks are strong, even extreme stress can be mitigated. Women often seem to maintain stronger social support networks than men, probably because of their primary involvement in childcare, a task that is made easier if shared among family or friends.

In the workplace   Social support is also utilised in the workplace, frequently being stronger among shop-floor employees than at management level. While social support at home is seen as having a useful function, this does not always generalise to the work situation; in the same way, social support at work does not often carry over to the home (van de Pompe and de Heus, 1993).

Traumatic events   Traumatic events, such as wars or earthquakes, produce strong feelings of cameraderie among those tryng to help the survivors, thereby reducing the stressful experience to a bearable level. This is another form of social support.

Defence mechanisms

Defence mechanisms were suggested by Freud as methods we employ to cope with anxiety and problems we do not wish to face directly. As such, these mechanisms preclude an individual from getting to grips with a problem and solving it. As these appear to have little or no physiological basis, they are only briefly described here.

1. **Avoidance**. The individual avoids the anxiety-provoking situation, in order not to experience stress. The social phobic avoids social situations, thereby fooling himself that he has no problems.
2. **Denial**. When a situation is too painful to face, an individual may deny that it simply exists. The wife of a terminally ill patient may refuse to accept that there is anything wrong, even though she has been given all the facts.
3. **Repression**. The problem is pushed into the unconscious so that it does not have to be dealt with.
4. **Projection**. The problem is projected to another person rather than being seen as one's own problem.
5. **Rationalisation**. The individual looks for logical reasons for the stressful situation. In fact, these may not appear logical to anyone else.
6. **Reaction formation**. Other thoughts or feelings are substituted, which are diametrically opposed to the truth. For example, a man may be experiencing stress because he is strongly attracted to his best friend's wife. In order to deal with this, he develops a hatred for her; this feeling causes less stress than does the strong attraction.

Maladaptive coping methods

Taking drugs and heavy drinking are regarded as maladaptive, in that they only mask the problem for a limited time. When the effect wears off, the stressor is still there. This is not the same as taking one drink to relax. A small amount of alcohol will depress activity in the CNS, as discussed in Chapter 3. This will reduce temporary arousal effectively but does not deal with ongoing stress.

Situation-focused coping

Cognitive appraisal

Problem-solving techniques are focused on the situation that is deemed to be causing stress. For example, driving to work down the motorway was proving very stressful; by leaving home five minutes earlier, I was able to drive to work along the B-roads, a much more pleasant way to start the day.

Time management

Not simply trying to cram too much into a day, but managing one's time ineffectively, is often a source of stress. Individuals can be taught to look at what has to be accomplished in a day, or a week, and find efficient ways of working so that they are not constantly backtracking and thereby wasting time. Establishing priorities and working to these is an efficient method of time management.

Assertiveness

Assertiveness training helps people to learn to say 'no' when imposed upon. They learn to ask for what they want without being aggressive or self-effacing. It is often a highly effective technique to counteract low self-esteem. This counteracts stress in several ways: by learning to say no, a person is not overworked or imposed upon; by asking for what they want, they are more likely to be happy with their situation; by seeing themselves as an effective person, they become more comfortable with themselves.

Other coping strategies

Relaxation and meditation

There is nothing really 'transcendental' about this. It is a specific technique that enables people to focus attention on specific thoughts. If attention is focused, it cannot wander and continually 'rehearse' worries and anxieties, which would raise arousal levels. Continually mentally rehearsing worries raises autonomic arousal. During relaxation, breathing is controlled, and heart rate and blood pressure are lowered.

Exercise

Exercise has been shown to be a highly effective form of stress management; even the physically unfit can reap the benefits by taking walks. It is thought that exercise shows two kinds of benefit in terms of relieving stress:

1. At the **physiological** level, it provides an outlet for the fight or flight responses, by providing physical activity.

2. At the **situational** level, it has the advantage of removing the individual from the stress-provoking situation.

Biofeedback

By teaching people how to lower their blood pressure and reduce other bodily symptoms of stress, it has been suggested that the harmful effects of stress may be counteracted. To date, few studies have shown conclusively that the beneficial effects are maintained outside the laboratory situation (see also Chapter 7, Section I). In addition, it has been argued that biofeedback is simply masking the experience of stress, not actually providing a respite.

SUMMARY

Anxiety and stress are distressing experiences for the individual; coping processes are usually invoked to reduce stress levels. Current models suggest that stress is the outcome of interaction between the person and an environment which that individual finds problematic. Individual differences between people may explain why we do not all recognise the same experiences as being stressful. Levels of social support available and positive coping methods also help to reduce the experience of stress.

SELF-ASSESSMENT QUESTIONS

1. Explain, with some examples, what is meant by the term 'stressors'.
2. Describe a physiological model of stress.
3. Outline an interactional model of stress.
4. Discuss some methods of coping with stress.

FURTHER READING

T. Cox, *Stress* (Basingstoke: Macmillan, 1978).

... And, for a perfect example of the way
non-stop partying affects the Circadian rhythms ...

Altered States of Consciousness 7

By the end of this chapter you will be able to:

- discuss different approaches to the concept of consciousness;
- describe altered states of consciousness and their implications;
- understand the relationship of biorhythms to pyschological states;
- describe the physiological processes involved in sleep; and
- outline theories which attempt to explain why humans sleep.

INTRODUCTION

Consciousness implies a state of awareness; altered states can vary from highly focused attention to the sleep state of dreaming. Although the sleep state may sound like a lack of consciousness, there are neural activities continuing and the sleeper can be roused, whereas in states of coma and persistent vegetative state (PVS) the individual cannot be roused.

SECTION I   LEVELS OF CONSCIOUSNESS

Unconscious, subconscious and preconscious

We sometimes say we have done a well-rehearsed action 'unconsciously'. Driving a car on a clear country road, or knitting, for example, does not occupy our full attention, but the action is not truly unconscious; it would be more correct to call it subconscious or preconscious, just below the level of conscious awareness. 'Unconscious' implies a total lack of awareness. If you are knocked out in the boxing ring or through an accident, you are unconscious.

Other psychologists may not agree with this definition of 'unconscious'; Freud, for example, viewed the unconscious mind as the repository for repressed memories. He suggested that the preconscious could become conscious if we switched our awareness to it.

These distinctions are not agreed by cognitive psychologists, who draw their conclusions from the level of mental processes during altered states of consciousness. Norman (1993) makes no distinction between preconscious and subconscious when discussing processes that are not wholly conscious. Hilgard (1977) suggests that we may use problem-solving abilities that are not always available to our conscious minds. You may have found that an answer sometimes pops into your head, yet you have no idea how you 'computed' it. The processing may have been subconscious, but the answer becomes conscious. Both may well have involved the cortex, which would suggest that not all cortical activities are necessarily conscious.

Neuropsychologists make distinctions between consciousness and unconsciousness on the basis of demonstrable activity within the nervous system through clinical observation. EEG, PET, CT and MRI scans contribute to this information. Objective information such as this has assisted in defining the difference between, for example, PVS and coma, but even this is limited and cannot always predict outcomes (prognosis).

Persistent vegetative state and coma

Persistent vegetative state (PVS) was brought to the public eye following the battle to allow Tony Bland to die. He had been a PVS patient for three and a half years, due to anoxia (lack of oxygen to the brain) suffered during the Hillsborough football stadium disaster. The term PVS was coined by Jennett and Plum (1972) to describe patients who appeared to recover from coma, showed periods of waking and sleeping, but never regained full cognitive functions. This state can appear after severe head injury or anoxia caused by asphxia, anaesthetic accidents, cardiac arrest, near-drowning or hypoglycaemia (unconsciousness caused by injecting too much insulin, which sometimes happens in diabetes) (Jennett, 1993).

To the ordinary observer, there is no ostensible difference between PVS and coma; the patients seem to be permanently unconscious, for months or years. Neurological investigations and clinical observations suggest that in PSV there is brainstem activity, which supports lower functions, such as breathing and the sleep/wake cycle, but little or no activity in the cortex, which is the region for higher processes such as information processing, problem solving and memory. If recovery from a vegetative state is to occur, it is most likely within the first year. After that time, it may be considered permanent (British Medical Association). However recent cases identified in 1996, where consciousness has been regained after two years or more, raises the questions of (a) whether the state was misdiagnosed originally, or (b) whether recovery is possible after a period of one year. At one time, very little treatment could be offered to PVS patients, but this is gradually changing (see Epilogue).

Coma usually follows severe head injury. Major neurological functions are disrupted. Usually within between two weeks and four months, functioning starts again spontaneously. Cortical functions such as visual tracking (following a moving object with the eyes), limb movement and vocalisations begin, together with reinstatement of the sleep/wake cycle. If these are not evident, vegetative state is suspected.

Consciousness

It does not seem possible to regard consciousness as a simple continuum, from high arousal at one end to deep sleep at the other. Where, along this continuum, would you place trance states or drug-induced states? Where does sleepwalking fit into our accepted idea of sleep as 'resting the body'? Certainly, consciousness must involve thought processes, memories and sensory inputs, but levels of all of these vary during states of consciousness. Kihlstrom (1984) suggests that the functions for which we use consciousness are:

1. monitoring ouselves and our environment, in order to make accurate cognitive representations; and
2. controlling our behaviour – when to begin and when to end specific behaviours and cognitive activities.

Awareness

It can be argued that awareness commences before a child is born. There is strong evidence that the foetus reacts to loud noise from outside the mother's body, and that external sound stimuli may affect later cognitive development. During childhood and adulthood, selective attention allows our awareness to be focused on specific stimuli (**focused attention**), while filtering out other events. You may be so engrossed in a book that you fail to hear or see what is going on around you. If someone says your name, however, you will hear it, because your **threshold of attention** is lower for this than for almost anything else. Other things around you, of which you are only vaguely aware, are within your **peripheral attention**. These can be brought into your focused attention at will, similar to the way in which Freud suggested that the preconscious can become conscious.

Habituation

Habituation occurs when a stimulus is so constant that it is no longer given conscious attention. Humans in urban societies become habituated to the constant noise of traffic. It would be detrimental to well-being to be constantly aware of and attending to that level of noise. Any change in the background noise immediatly raises conscious awareness. Habituation, therefore, has survival value.

EEG patterns can reflect the neural state of habituation. If a stimulus is introduced, the EEG pattern is disrupted to reflect the introduction of the stimulus.

There are so many stimuli around us that do not gain our conscious (focal) attention, to which we may say we are habituated. We are not unconscious of them; perhaps it would be more correct to say they are in our preconscious or subconscious, our peripheral attention.

Suggestibility and hypnosis

In a highly aware state, the cognitive processes may be very active, examining and analysing incoming stimuli. In a more relaxed state, these processes are less focused and therefore more open to **suggestibility** or receptive to suggestions from others. It is with this state that **hypnotists** work, placing suggestions into receptive minds. The voice of the hypnotist becomes the focus of attention and other stimuli are filtered out.

Hypnotised subjects are not 'asleep', as is the common concept. The hypnotic state is nothing like sleepwalking. In many therapies that use hypnosis (for enabling people to give up smoking, for example), the client is conscious but relaxed, listening only to the hypnotist. An association is formed between the pleasant feeling of the relaxed state, the soothing voice of the hypnotist and the suggestion that the client no longer desires or needs to smoke in order to feel relaxed.

Hypnosis is used to allow people to openly recall memories that they have repressed as being painful. Recalling incidents of abuse as a child is an example that has received much publicity; in some cases, doubt has been cast on whether the incident was recalled by the client or suggested by the hypnotist, as the client is obviously so open to suggestion.

Deeper states of hypnosis are sometimes achieved, as in stage hypnosis, in which people act in ways that seem out of character and later cannot remember what they did while hypnotised. The ethics of inducing these states simply for the entertainment of others is questionable, and whether there are long-term repercussions for the individual concerned is an area that has not been researched. It is highly unlikely that an individual could be hypnotised to commit any action to which he or she was completely opposed (for example assault or murder), even under deep hypnosis.

In other instances, hypnosis has been used instead of anaesthetic during operations. Patients reported no experience of pain, and bleeding was reduced.

There are a number of suggestions offered as to what happens to the individual during hypnosis. One suggestion is that subjects or clients are simply being compliant, that they are 'going along' with the hypnotist. Orne (1979) suggested an extension of this idea: that the hypnotist is actually changing the client's motivational state. Hilgard (1977) views hypnosis as being a dissociative state, in the same way that an individual with multiple personalities would slip into a different personality and have no thought or feeling, or even knowledge, of the 'other self'. Clinical and experimental evidence has so far produced conflicting results on whether any suggestion so far proposed is correct.

Meditation and trance states

Meditation has been practised by humans for thousands of years and is strongly associated with many Eastern religions and traditions. During meditation, the attention is strongly focused on a stimulus, either external, such as the tip of a candle flame, or internal, such as the repetition of a mantra, words or phrases that have a rhythm and are designed to bring the individual to a higher level of consciousness. In the religious context, the aim is to bring the person nearer to high levels of selflessness, transcending the bodily state.

During meditation, all extraneous stimuli are excluded, the heart rate and breathing rate slow, and blood pressure and basal metabolic rate drop. The body is immobilised and therefore its physical demands are reduced to the lowest levels, enabling fasting to be carried out for long periods of time. The physical processes of the body are all rested by the process of meditation; relaxation also achieves this but not so deeply and completely. Devotees of meditation say that they feel more refreshed after half an hour's meditation than after a night's sleep; this is obviously achieved only by practice. This assertion would seem reasonable, in that during sleep the body is not always immobilised, and the brain may be more active than when simply repeating a mantra.

Trance states have been observed in individuals from a number of different cultures. During trance, it is suggested, the individual's 'mind' is no longer within the body. This is a much more difficult state to define or prove objectively. In many cultures, those who exhibit trance states are revered, and their pronouncements while in a trance are accepted as messages from gods or people who have died. Again, very little scientific investigation has been conducted on trance states, although no one denies that they happen. It may be that the 'messages' are a product of the individuals' own thought processes of which they are not consciously aware.

Drug-induced states

Since reading Chapter 3, where the action of drugs is briefly explained, the reader will not be expecting transcendental explanations for drug states. The explanation for changes in perception, feelings and experiences is wholly chemical, mainly due to chemical changes at the synapse, thereby sending false messages to the cognitive parts of the brain. These false messages are responsible for people's out-of-character actions while under the influence of drugs.

Epilepsy

Epileptic attacks can range from brief apparent lapses of attention to intense electrical activity in the brain, causing unconsciousness and severe muscular contractions. Anyone might have an attack, if sufficiently provoked; some years ago, stroboscopes were implicated as causing changes in the electical activity of the brain, because of the rhythmical changes in their light patterns. Experiencing one seizure does not therefore necessarily denote epilepsy; people with epilepsy have a low **seizure threshold**. Partial seizures, as the name implies, involve only part of the brain and are usually confined to one hemisphere. Generalised seizures involve both hemispheres. Seizures usually emanate from a focal point, which is often difficult to locate, whether by EEG or scans; 30–40 per cent occur in the temporal lobe.

Causes of epilepsy may be **symptomatic** – related to some definable brain injury or deformity, or infection such as meningitis. The majority of cases of epilepsy are idiopathic – there appears to be no specific cause, although some genetic factors have been demonstrated. Some cases of epilepsy have been linked to drug abuse, emotional disturbances and hormonal changes, such as those occurring during adolescence. Epilepsy is usually controllable by such drugs as phenytoin or nitrazepam.

Sensory deprivation

The brain normally has a continuous input of stimuli, which is attended or rejected, responded to or 'filed'. If all stimuli cease, the brain is then in an abnormal state and may attempt to fill this vacuum with stimuli of its own making – hallucinations. Even if external stimuli are cut off, the chemical activity of the brain cannot be switched off like a light bulb.

Sensory deprivation experiments involve people in wearing headgear that cuts off sound and vision, and floating in a tank of body-heat water, which deprives the remaining senses. Subjects soon begin to hallucinate, accusing their researchers of 'talking about them', or other imaginary experiences; when they become distressed, usually within a few hours, the experiment is halted.

Partial sensory deprivation for a short period of time has been used therapeutically for those who lead high-stress lifestyles. However the deprivation is not total, as soothing music is played to them. The aim is to reduce their sensory input for a time, rather than have them experience total deprivation.

Biofeedback

Biofeedback is the term used for a technique that aims to teach people consciously to control their autonomic processes; parameters such as heart rate and blood pressure are normally regulated without conscious control.

If a person has high blood pressure, for example, which causes health problems, it is advantageous to reduce this. Patients are connected to apparatus that continuously records their blood pressure, and they may a conscious effort to reduce it. When it drops below the target level, a buzzer sounds; this is reinforcement for the individual, knowing that a step towards health has been achieved. However, maintenance of the improvement is rarely achieved after training sessions cease. Blanchard *et al.* (1979) found relaxation training to be more successful than biofeedback. Neuromuscular disorders, such as cerebral palsy, have been treated by biofeedback (Basmajian, 1977). Neural pathways that are normally under voluntary control, but have been disordered, should be ideal for retraining. Patients are informed by biofeedback of the firing of single-nerve muscle cells and trained to reactivate these. In damaged tissue, signs of muscle movement are faint and need amplification; this acts as reinforcement and a prompt for further effort.

Summary

When we speak of consciousness, we are describing a state of cortical awareness. Even this may be divided into **focal attention**, where the concentration lies, and **peripheral attention**, other things that can be brought into focal attention at will.

Subconscious (or preconscious) processes may include not only an awareness of what is within our peripheral attention, but also **habituated responses** that we make, without reference to our conscious mind. Again, these may be brought into consciousness at will, or if the circumstances of these responses evoke a change. Other processes, which we can only call subconscious for want of a better term, are those which cannot always be accessed by the conscious mind, for example, the problem-solving abilities described by Hilgard.

The **unconscious** state implies lack of consciousness. Unfortunately, this term is used to describe other states, so terminology needs to be standardised. Unconscious states range from temporary loss of consciousness, to coma and vegetative states. PVS patients may show some brainstem activity, but little or no cortical functioning.

Self-assessment questions

1. What is meant by 'altered states of consciousness'?
2. How do we define awareness?
3. Briefly describe and contrast two altered states of consciousness from those discussed so far.

SECTION II   BODY RHYTHMS

Biorhythms

The human body exhibits a number of regular, recognisable rhythms, the most noticeable of which is the **circadian rhythm**.

This term comes from the Latin *circa*, meaning 'about' and *dies*, meaning 'a day'. Circadian rhythms are those which we exhibit throughout the day, sleep being the most obvious because it takes up approximately one third of our 24-hour day. Most animals also exhibit a circadian rhythm, even when they are **nocturnal** (active by night rather than by day).

Other body rhythms may take more than a day to be repeated, for example the menstrual cycle (approximately 28 days). These are called **infradian rhythms**, from the Latin *infra*, meaning below; these cycles occurring less often than once a day. Hibernation in some animals is another example of an infradian rhythm; it takes months to reoccur.

Some body rhythms occur more than once a day. These are called **ultradian rhythms**, from the Latin word *ultra*, meaning above or over. Rhythms that occur more than once a day include the hunger 'cycle', usually about every four hours in Western society. Sleep, while being part of the circadian rhythm, also itself contains these less-than-a-day rhythms – stages within the pattern of sleep.

Circadian rhythms

Does our body have a natural 24-hour rhythm, or is this only due to the light/dark cycle of our planet? If we lived in 24-hour 'light', would our bodies still produce the same rhythm? These were some of the questions scientists aimed to answer when, in 1972, a French caver called Siffre volunteered to spend seven months underground. He had adequate food, water and books, and a telephone link to the outside world. He was monitored by video camera and computer. He established a pattern of existence without cues as to time or the light/dark cycle.

The cycle that he established was approximately 25 hours, one hour longer than the circadian rhythm which has access to light/dark cues. This demonstrated that people have an innate mechanism for the circadian rhythm that will continue to function in the absence of daylight.

This begs the question of whether blind people are experiencing a longer-cycle circadian rhythm than sighted people. Miles *et al.* (1977) report the case of a young, professional man who had been blind from birth. He had a circadian rhythm of 24.9 hours. In order to stay in phase with the rest of society, he had to take doses of stimulants and sedatives at appropriate times. Attempts to shift his sleep/wake cycle by controlling his sleep pattern in a laboratory were unsuccessful.

Disruption of the circadian rhythm

If the circadian rhythm is disrupted, for example by flying to another part of the world, so that we land in a different time zone from that of where we took off, the body has to readjust. Sleep has to be reinstated at a different time, as do eating patterns.

What is not so obvious is that our other patterns have been disrupted. For example, during the night not only does a person sleep, but also the breathing rate and heart rate slow considerably, and body temperature and blood pressure both drop. All these have to be changed. If you are staying for a fortnight's holiday, it may take you a few days to 'feel right' after your experience of jet-lag. Pilots, who are constantly flying across time zones, tend to ignore local times and keep to their own body clocks. The circadian rhythm seems to adapt more easily when travelling from east to west, rather than from west to east, possibly because our innate rhythm may be 25-hour, and we can make the adaptation more easily.

Shift work

With this in mind, what happens to the body when an individual has to do shift work? A study with nurses, moving from day-shift to night-shift, found that for some nurses, it took almost a full week for body mechanisms to readjust and function as if it were daytime (Hawkins and Armstong-Esther, 1978).

The implications of these and other findings would seem to recommend that shift changes should be for longer than a week (perhaps three to four weeks) and that shifts should be rotated clockwise. Workers who rotate shifts weekly have more accidents at work, show lower productivity, and experience insomnia, digestive problems, fatigue and psychosomatic illnesses such as depression, owing to the individual's body being under stress. In spite of this evidence, there are still major companies today who are running weekly shifts that rotate anticlockwise!

Hormonal causes governing the menstrual cycle were described in Chapter 4. Other biological mechanisms involved in running the body's biorhythms will be discussed in the next section.

Summary

The human body exhibits innate biorhythms. Some are circadian rhythms, centred around the light/dark cycle; others are greater than a day, such as the menstrual cycle in women, or less than a day, such as stages within a night's sleep. Disruption of these body rhythms causes stress to the body, which has to readjust to new patterns.

Self-assessment questions

1. What are biorhythms?
2. What are the physiological consequences of disrupting the circadian rhythms?
3. What are some possible behavioural consequences of disrupting the circadian rhythms?

SECTION III   THE RHYTHMS OF SLEEP

Sleep is an altered state of consciousness; it is by no means a total lack of consciousness, as external stimuli (such as loud noises) filter through and may be incorporated into any ongoing neural activity, for example dreams. Additionally, it is possible to rouse a person from sleep, whereas it is not possible to rouse someone who is unconscious.

Sleep is part of the circadian rhythm; it happens once in 24 hours (excluding catnaps). During sleep, ultradian rhythms emerge as different stages of sleep succeed each other. These are identifiable and definable by EEG patterns and, in the instance of dream sleep, by observation. In this section, we shall be looking at the physiological processes of sleep, and stages of sleep.

Physiology of sleep

In birds and reptiles, the **pineal organ**, situated in the brain, has receptors that are directly stimulated by light, which can penetrate the thin layer of skull above the pineal. This gives the first clue as to whether it is time to sleep or to wake. In humans, the **pineal gland** is situated deeper in the brain, at the top of the brainstem. Projections carrying nervous impulses from the retina bring light/dark information to the pineal. The pineal secretes **melatonin**; more seems to be produced in response to fading light.

The melatonin produced by the pineal gland acts upon the **raphe nuclei** (a group of cells situated in the pons, see Figure 7.1), which produce **serotonin**, a neurotransmitter with an inhibitory, or slowing down, effect on the CNS, particularly in the region of the reticular formation, which is known as one of the body's arousal systems.

FIGURE 7.1
Summary diagram showing regions of the brain that have been reported to be involved in controlling arousal or sleep

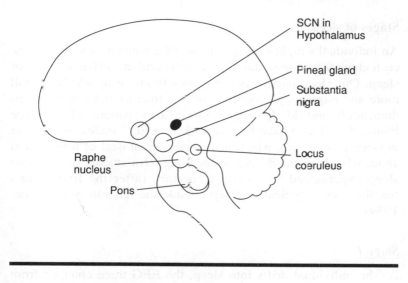

SCN in Hypothalamus

Pineal gland

Substantia nigra

Locus coeruleus

Raphe nucleus

Pons

However, the key pacemaker of the circadian rhythm seems to be the **supra-chiasmatic nucleus** (SCN), in the hypothalamus.

This contains around 10 000 small neurons (Meijer and Reitveld, 1989), which synapse onto each other and are thought to be neurosecretory cells that may send neuromodulators to influence many areas of the brain. The projections from the retina to the pineal gland come via the SCN, but this is not the main method of maintaining the circadian rhythm. As Siffre had shown, it can be maintained in the absence of a light/dark cycle. The neurones of the SCN display an endogenous (inbuilt) circadian rhythm. If the nucleus is damaged, the circadian rhythm becomes disorganised. The SCN also sends projections to the raphe nuclei, which, we have already shown, is involved in the circadian cycle.

Also involved in the sleep/wake cycle are a group of neurones known as the **locus coerulus**, situated in the reticular formation. The rate of firing of these neurones declines just before sleep and increases abruptly just before waking (Aston-Jones and Bloom, 1981), indicating that they may be involved in vigilance rather than the sleep/wake cycle. It is thought that these neurones also play a role in **REM sleep** (rapid eye movement sleep, usually indicative of dreaming), as their rate of firing drops to zero during REM.

Stages of sleep

An individual's night's sleep consists of a number of sleep cycles, each about 90 minutes' duration, which combine different levels of sleep. Our sleep pattern is not a smooth curve in which we fall more and more deeply asleep until it is time to wake again. Children, adults and elderly people show different patterns of sleep (see Figure 7.2). These have been recorded on EEG traces, as they are in sleep laboratories, which has given a great deal of information about what happens during sleep. Long-term studies suggest that sleep experienced in a sleep laboratory (after the first night's 'settling-in') is typical of sleep outside the laboratory (Empson, 1989).

Stage 1

As the individual drifts into sleep, the EEG trace changes from the recognisable **alpha rhythm**, which characterises the relaxed waking state (see Figure 7.3), to the irregular trace of Stage 1 sleep. The EEG demonstrates low-voltage, slow waves (2–7 Hz, low amplitude). The individual is easily woken during this stage. Other physiological changes begin: the heart rate and breathing rate begin to slow down.

FIGURE 7.2
Normal sleep cycles of humans at different ages

Dreaming episodes are indicated by black bars. Note the deeper sleep of children and more frequent periods of waking in the elderly. Sleep stages are judged by EEG criteria.

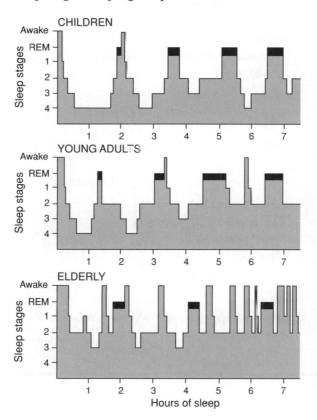

Source: Kales and Kales (1974)

FIGURE 7.3
Typical EEG traces for (NREM) stages of sleep and REM sleep

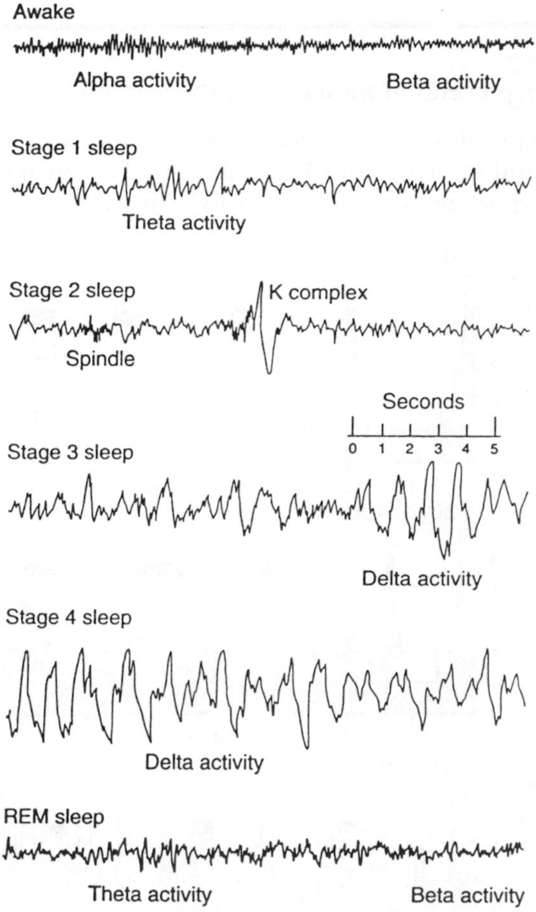

Source: Horne (1988)

Stage 2

The EEG trace is of higher amplitude and shows characteristic 'spindle' patterns, of 13–15 Hz, which last for about 20 seconds.

The reason for these is not known; they do not appear to correspond with any overt behavioural changes (such as turning over, for example). The individual is still quite easily awoken at this stage.

Stage 3

The individual is difficult to rouse during this stage, a behavioural indication of deeper sleep. A stimulus important to the individual will break the barrier; for example, a mother will hear her baby cry and wake up, whereas other stimuli of the same noise level may have no effect. The sleeper's heart rate and breathing rate are slow, and blood pressure drops. The EEG trace shows long, slow waves.

Stage 4

As for Stage 3, the sleeper can only be roused with difficulty, except for relevant stimuli. Heart rate and breathing rate are slow, and blood pressure is lowered. The EEG trace shows long, slow, rhythmical waves.

Within the first three and a half hours of a night's sleep, an individual has probably completed all the 'deep' sleep (Stages 3 and 4) that is likely to occur. Subsequent sleep cycles are likely to fluctuate between Stages 1 and 2. In most normal people, all sleep cycles include a period of REM sleep.

REM sleep and dreaming

Rapid eye movement (REM) sleep was first identified by Dement and Kleitman (1957). They observed subjects in a sleep laboratory who showed periods of sleep when their eyes could be observed rapidly moving under their lids. Eye movements can be monitored and recorded by an **electro-oculogram** (EOG), a process similar to an EEG but recording from near the eye socket.

If the volunteers were woken when their eyes showed rapid movements, they reported that they were dreaming. This happened 80 per cent of the time, whereas if subjects were woken during non-REM (**NREM**) sleep, they reported dreams only 15 per cent of the time. However, Beaumont (1988) suggests that subjects take longer to rouse from NREM sleep and may therefore have forgotten their dreams by the time they are fully awake and coherent.

Bursts of dreaming during REM may only last for a few seconds, with quiescent periods in between. In recall, however, we may link these bursts together, to form one dream, which may account for some of the inconsistencies and irrelevances we recall in our dreams.

Newborn babies spend much of their sleep time in REM sleep. Unfortunately, it is impossible to establish whether they experience dreams at this time, and if so, of what they are dreaming.

Faraday (1973) found that the rapidity of the eye movements correlated with the intensity of the dream. In addition, movements of the inner ear occur, which may be related to the auditory content of the dreams. This may be why we sometimes incorporate external noises into our dreams.

As stated earlier, neurones in the locus coeruleus fire during REM sleep. These prompt another important physiological mechanism, the inhibition of motoneurones in the brainstem, in order to cut off physical activity from mental activity, so that individuals do not act out their dreams.

Sleep deprivation studies

It has been found impossible to keep human subjects awake continually. They take microsleeps, or even fall asleep standing up!

The longest recorded period of wakefulness was 264 hours. This was completed by a young disc jockey, who stayed on air for that period of time. He was carefully monitored for well-being during the experience. At no time did he lose touch with reality, although he experienced some minor illusions and psychological problems. After approximately 250 hours, his body temperature was 1^0C below normal and his skin temperature $10\ ^0$C below normal, indicating that the capillaries were constricting to conserve body heat.

Tests of mental functioning showed some decrement, especially speech and memory. Eye and motor control showed impairment at times. His circadian rhythm was still evident during deprivation.

His sleep was monitored for three nights following deprivation. Results showed that the first night's sleep showed a great increase in Stage 4 and REM sleep. This pattern was followed on the two subsequent nights, indicating that these are areas important in sleep.

This is, of course, a case study and may not generalise to the population at large. Other studies have tended selectively to deprive people of either REM or NREM sleep (Dement, 1960, 1972). Findings generally suggest that REM sleep is increased following a period of deprivation. Dement's earlier study suggested that REM sleep-deprived subjects displayed a form of paranoia, but his later study did not find this.

Webb (1982) found that if volunteers were asked gradually to reduce their period of sleep from eight to four hours per night over a period of two months, they appeared to suffer no detrimental effect. In a previous experiment, Webb had asked participants to abruptly reduce their sleep to three hours per night for eight nights. Deterioration on cognitive and performance tasks was apparent by the seventh night.

It would appear from experimental studies that, while humans need sleep in order to function effectively, cognition and performance are unaffected by controlled sleep reduction. However, the volunteers are usually young, fit adults, and the experimental period is predetermined, which may enhance their motivation.

REM rebound

If people are deprived of REM sleep during one night, their following night's sleep will contain longer periods of REM, as though they have a need to 'catch up'. This phenomenon is known as **REM rebound**.

NREM and dreams

Subjects woken during NREM reported shorter, less visual dreams. However, these were sometimes of the 'nightmare' type of dream, in which there was a strong emotional outburst. Sleep-walking (somnambulism) and sleeptalking occur during NREM sleep Where dreams are sometimes 'acted out', these may be of the NREM variety, as they are usually linked to some highly emotional experience, and of course the motor neurones are not inhibited at these stages.

Summary

Specific structures in the brain have been found to be involved with aspects of sleep. Activity in the cortex during sleep can be monitored noninvasively by EEG recordings. Differences in these traces indicate when sleep is changing from one stage to another. Cycles of sleep (ultradian rhythms) last about 90 minutes and normally include several stages of sleep in each cycle. REM sleep usually indicates dreaming.

There seems to be evidence that sleep, rather than quiet rest, is necessary for human well-being. When volunteers are allowed less than four hours sleep per night, their cognitive functions show decrement within a week. If this were to be prolonged beyond the usual experimental period, other problems might become evident. REM sleep seems to be of particular importance: people deprived of REM sleep increase the proportion of time spent in REM on subsequent nights.

Self-assessment questions

1. Describe some important physiological processes involved in sleep.
2. What are the differences between REM and NREM sleep?
3. Describe an example of an ultradian rhythm.
4. (a) What do sleep deprivation studies show?
   (b) Why must this information be viewed with caution?

SECTION IV   WHY DO WE SLEEP?

In this section, we shall be trying to answer the question of why we need to sleep and also to dream. These questions have been addressed by a number of researchers, who have formulated theories of sleep and dreaming. Given that we, as humans, need to rest in order not to exhaust ourselves, why do we need to sleep instead of just sitting or lying quietly?

All animals sleep, even though the process may leave them open to attack by predators. For example, the Indus dolphin, which is blind, sleeps for approximately seven hours a day – in 'naps' of 4–60 seconds! (Pilleri, 1979). Other marine mammals exhibit similar patterns, suggesting that sleep is a physiological necessity.

THEORIES OF SLEEP

Restoration theory

Oswald (1980) proposed that sleep is the period of quiescence necessary for the body and brain to replenish themselves, to repair any deterioration and damage sustained during the day. Body replenishment, he suggested, occurs during NREM sleep, and brain replenishment during REM sleep.

Physiological evidence is offered in support of this theory. In normal adults, **growth hormone** is only secreted during slow wave (NREM) sleep. In children, there is also some secretion occurring during the day. While growth hormone is obviously important in children (especially young babies), it also has a function in adults. Growth hormone increases the ability of amino acids (the constituents of proteins) to enter body cells. Assisting the process of **restoration of body tissue** is important, because cells need to be renewed regularly and frequently.

However, critics have pointed out that amino acids are only readily available for four hours after a meal, so not a great deal of protein synthesis will take place at night, during fasting. Studies have demonstrated that the rate of protein synthesis is higher during the day than at night (Clugston and Garlick, 1982). A human's metabolic rate is only 9 per cent lower during sleep than during quiet wakefulness; therefore a great deal of our potential for cell replenishment occurs by day.

The restoration of brain tissue during REM sleep would seem to imply the necessity for a period of quiescence in order for repair to be carried out, but, as we have seen earlier, the brain is extremely active during REM sleep.

Evolutionary theory

Meddis (1983) proposed that the need for sleep is rooted in our evolutionary past. Sleep is an advantage because it keeps the animal immobilised and inconspicuous for long periods of time. Because it is inconspicuous, it is therefore out of danger from predators.

Animals who are unlikely to be in danger from predators, such as lions, can sleep quite openly during the day. Other species, such as the Indus dolphin mentioned at the start of this section, have to adapt their sleep patterns. Humans, although predatory rather than hunted, sleep at night because human sight, unlike that of members of the cat family for example, is not specialised for seeing in the dark.

Herd animals, such as zebra, usually sleep standing up (they do not fall over, as humans would, because they have a suspensory ligament in their legs that keeps them rigid during sleep). Many herd animals take microsleeps or short naps. Additionally, in a herd, there are usually some individuals awake while others sleep.

Because of this evolutionary predispositon to sleep, Meddis argues, people have maintained this behaviour, even though it may seem largely unnecessary in an urbanised society, to be immobilised against danger. There are functional benefits, in that the long sleeps that babies have prevent their mothers from being exhausted.

This theory would seem to suggest that sleep is not necessary in a safe environment. Animal studies (for example Kleitman, 1927) showed that death eventually results from lack of sleep. Human sleep deprivation studies show that people deprived of sleep will sleep marginally more after deprivation, with a marked increase in the percentage of REM sleep, as though they need to 'catch up'.

Hibernation theory

Seemingly a variation on evolutionary theory, hibernation theory suggests that sleep evolved as a lesser form of hibernation, with the purpose of keeping humans and animals quiet and immobilised in the dark. Hibernating animals are also conserving energy and not using up food stores, or pointlessly looking for food in a season when none is available. If humans did not sleep at night, they would probably need to consume more food, which would deplete available resources.

There is not a great deal of support for hibernation theory. Other evolutionary behaviours that are not necessary for survival or lifestyle have been minimised or discarded by humans. It is unlikely that the species as a whole would seek to maintain a behaviour that occupies one third of human life but has no real purpose.

Core sleep and optional sleep

Horne (1988) suggested that, while we need sleep, we mostly have more sleep than is necessary.

He discounted Oswald's restoration theory on the basis that cell restoration takes place by day rather than at night. He also suggested that the increase in growth hormone at night might be related to the breakdown of fat rather than to protein synthesis.

Horne suggests that the first four hours of sleep are **core sleep**, which are necessary for rest, relaxation and restitution of the brain. The remaining hours of sleep he terms **optional sleep**, as these can be dispensed with, to no ill-effect.

Horne cites a study by Wilkinson, who allowed three groups of participants 4, 6 and 7.5 hours of sleep per night respectively, for six weeks. The cognitive functioning of participants was tested before and after this period of time. The 6- and 7.5-hour groups showed no decrement in cognitive functions, whereas the 4-hour group showed some decrement in memory. Horne concluded that no more than five hours of sleep was physiologically necessary. Any additional hours spent asleep were just an acquired habit.

If you refer back to Figure 7.2, you will see that, by the end of four hours sleep, an adult has completed all of the slow wave sleep for the night, plus less than half of the REM sleep. Horne would therefore seem to be suggesting that not all of the REM sleep is necessary. Most studies have shown that the long-term deprivation of REM sleep, when people are on sleeping tablets for example, is extremely detrimental and may result in hallucinations and other mental health problems.

THEORIES OF DREAMING

If one of the reasons why we sleep is to allow us to dream, we should examine the reasons why we dream. If a sleeper is woken during REM sleep, he or she can recall the ongoing dream, so the dream state cannot be far from conscious awareness; it is another level of consciousness. Researchers have not yet clarified whether REM sleep is solely for the purpose of dreaming, and also why we need to dream. We will look at a few theories.

Psychoanalytic theories

Freud's theory of dreams

In perhaps the best known, yet least scientifically based theory, Freud suggested that dreams are wish fulfillment. Those things which we would like but cannot have in real life are the things we dream about. Some which we cannot admit, even to ourselves, are disguised and need interpretation by a therapist.

Jung's theory of dreams

Jung suggested that dreams should be analysed in series rather than as individual dreams; a single dream would give little information on the dreamer's problems.

The lack of empirical data, or methods of finding empirical data, to substantiate psychoanalytic dream theories makes them difficult to accept. The interpretation of dreams by a therapist may be construed as being not entirely objective.

In addition, dreams can only be recorded by self-report, which is not an objective method. People may inadvertently add to their recalled dream, to include their current problem. Perhaps examining the content of dreams is not the most useful route to determining why we dream.

Neurological theories

Rose's neural theory

Rose (1976) explained dreams as the output from the brain's random firings. These random firings may trigger memory sequences, which are then strung together as dreams. It is not really determined why some memory sequences and not others are triggered, or why dreams may contain hitherto unknown places or people.

Activation–synthesis model

This model was proposed by Hobson and McCarley (1977). The high level of cortical activity during REM is not input from the senses but is internally generated, a form of 'neural noise'. This is the **activation** part of the model. **Synthesis** is the interpretation of this neural activity into dream sequences. Each individual synthesises his or her dreams according to their unique experiences. Genuine physiological input is incorporated into the dream. For example, the brainstem blocking of motor activity is recognised in the dream as trying to run away but being unable to do so.

The authors propose that this process occurs during REM sleep. There seems to be no reason why the process is postponed during NREM. Random firings are probably still generated and passed to the cortex during NREM sleep, and may also be synthesised into dreams.

Forgetting theory

Crick and Mitchison (1983) suggested that, during sleep, the cortex receives input from the brainstem during which synapses are modified so that unwanted connections are 'unlearned'. The function of REM, they suggest, is to sort and discard, or forget, unwanted learning. The exact mechanism for this selection and disconnection is as yet unidentified.

The perceptual content of our dreams corresponds with the activity generated in the perceptual cortex. The frontal lobes of the brain are probably involved in weaving this perceptual input into a story. This may account for why some people's dreams are more creative than others!

Hopfield (1984) carried out some computer-simulation experiments, with 'learning computers', as described in Chapter 3. These simulate human learning processes, using connectionist models. Hopfield found that if a learning computer had been given superfluous information, it consolidated its necessary information more efficiently if given a period of unlearning of unnecessary information. This would seem to be similar to the process that Crick and Mitchison thought to occur in humans.

Reorganisation of mental structures

Ornstein (1986) suggests that REM sleep and dreaming may be involved in consolidating learning. This time is used by the brain to reorganise its mental structures into a memorable form. Support for this comes from experimental evidence that shows that REM sleep increases after people have been asked to learn complex tasks.

This process has been suggested, by some writers, as the reason why newborns spend so much time in REM sleep (50 per cent as opposed to an adult's 25 per cent, of sleep time). This seems behaviourally unlikely, as a newborn may only be awake for half an hour, feeding, then asleep for a further three hours. That would give one and a half hours processing time for half an hour's information input. It seems unlikely that the function of a newborn's REM sleep is the same as that of an adult, unless the actual functions of REM are very different from those already proposed.

SUMMARY

In this section, we have looked at both theories of sleep and theories of dreaming. Some theories of sleep suggest that humans need sleep time for body and brain restitution. Others suggest that it is a behavioural carry-over from our evolutionary past. As adults, humans spend approximately 25 per cent of their sleep time in REM sleep, which researchers have found to be associated with dreaming. Reasons given for dreaming range from the emotional expression of wishes to the random firings of brain cells. Functions suggested for these random firings may be associated with learning: either the consolidation of learning or the sorting and forgetting of unwanted information.

Although a great deal of information has been uncovered on the physiological processes of sleep, answers to questions such as why we sleep and why we dream are as yet still open to discussion. This is what makes psychology so interesting; when we know all the answers, I shall give it up and take up knitting or nuclear physics!

SELF-ASSESSMENT QUESTIONS

1. (a) Describe the restoration theory of sleep.
   (b) What are the criticisms of this theory?
2. What other suggestions have been made for the reason why humans sleep?
3. What are the problems associated with the psychoanalytic theories of dreaming?
4. Briefly compare and contrast two neurological theories of REM sleep.

FURTHER READING

E Hilgard, *Divided Consciousness: Multiple controls in human thought and action.* (New York: Wiley, 1977).

J. Horne, *Why We Sleep: The functions of sleep in humans and other mammals.* (Oxford: Oxford University Press, 1988).

Epilogue

In this book, I have tried to give the reader some insight into the mind/body relationship, based on our current understanding of how the body 'works', together with how mental processes appear to relate to these physical processes. Through constraints of book size, I have only been able to look at a few specific areas of knowledge. There are more, and I hope the reader's appetite will have been whetted to search these out.

In some areas, the knowledge base is being extended almost day by day. There are exciting new developments occurring in physiological psychology and its associated fields of cognitive science and neuropsychology.

The field of computer modelling of cognitive processes has been mentioned in this book. This area is giving useful insights to psychologists from many disciplines into the ways in which human learning may occur. Its premise has also been utilised to **rehabilitate** patients after brain injury. As human beings, we never stop learning; if the brain can be re-educated to process information in new ways, forming new neural networks to replace those which are damaged or useless, skills may be relearned which were previously thought impossible. This has tremendous implications for people injured in accidents – and their relatives.

Increased knowledge of the biochemical functioning of the brain has led to advances in **neuropharmacology**. New drugs and new treatments are being used to treat people with mental problems that have demonstrable physiological causes. The quality of life is improved tremendously for a number of these people, which is what treatment is all about – not just sustaining life, but improving it.

Increased knowledge of brain physiology and functioning has led to pioneering work in the field of **neural transplants**. Early work carried out in Sweden showed that Parkinson's disease (due to deterioration of the dopamine-producing neurones) could be alleviated by transplanting such cells from a foetus into an adult brain. Foetal cells were used in order to overcome the problems of tissue rejection. However, if a healthy neurone could be removed from an individual, and perhaps grown in culture, and then retransplanted into that same person, both ethical questions and the practical problems of rejection would be resolved at the same time.

These new fields, at the cutting edge of science, raise new practical, ethical and philosophical questions, which must be addressed. If it can be demonstrated that rehabilitation can be brought about even after severe brain injury, to provide an acceptable quality of life, what are the new criteria for keeping people alive on life-support machines? The practical implications of provision of treatment, and costs, will have to be considered, as must support systems to alleviate the psychological stress imposed on that individual's family.

The same sorts of problem arise in individuals on drug therapies. Their treatments may be expensive; their families will now, of necessity, be involved in their care, as there are currently few long-stay psychiatric hospital places. Is there a more than evens chance that their quality of life will be improved by their treatment? With the advances made in science in recent years, the answer is 'yes', provided the practicalities can keep up with science.

The ethical question of using aborted foetuses for neural transplants is one that raises many arguments. Emotively it is argued, these are living humans who should not be used for 'spare parts'. On the other hand, if they are to die anyway, should they not help to improve the quality of life for someone else? However, recent progress made in tissue cultures may remove the need to use foetal cells.

New horizons in science – especially the human sciences – are bound to raise new ethical, practical and philosophical questions, which will need to be met as they arise. Meanwhile, the frontiers of knowledge are still being pushed back. We live in an exciting age.

Bibliography

Adams, A. (1992) *Bullying at Work*. London: Virago Press.

Adams, D.B. (1979) Brain mechanisms for offense, defense and submission, *Behavioral and Brain Science*, **2**, 201–41.

Adams, D.B. (1986) Ventomedial tegmental lesions abolish offense without disturbing predation or defense, *Physiology and Behavior*, **38**, 165–8.

Anand, B.K. and Brobeck, J.R. (1951) Hypothalamic control of food intake in rats and cats, *Yale Journal of Biology and Medicine*, **24**, 123–40.

Animals (Scientific Procedures) Act (1986) London: HMSO.

Artmann, H., Grau, H., Adelman, M. and Schleiffer, R. (1985) Reversible and non-reversible enlargement of cerebrospinal fluid spaces in anorexia nervosa, *Neuroradiology*, **27**, 103–12.

Aston-Jones, G. and Bloom, F.E. (1981) Activity of norepinephrine-containing locus coeruleus neurons in behaving rats anticipates fluctuations in the sleep-waking cycle, *Journal of Neuroscience*, **1**, 876–86.

Atkinson, R.L., Atkinson R.C., Smith, E.E. and Hilgard, E.R. (1987) *Introduction to Psychology* (9th edn). Orlando: Harcourt Brace Jovanovich.

Averill, J.R. (1983) Studies on anger and aggression: implications for theories of emotion, *American Psychologist*, **38**, 1145–60.

Ax, A.F. (1953) The physiological differentiation of fear and anger in humans, *Psychosomatic Medicine*, **15**, 433–42.

Bandura, A., Ross, D. and Ross, S.A. (1963) Imitation of film-mediated aggressive models, *Journal of Abnormal and Social Psychology*, **66**, 3–11.

195

Basmajian, J.V. (1977) Learned control of single motor units, in G.E. Schwartz and J. Beatty (eds), *Biofeedback: Theory and research*. New York: Academic Press.

Baylis, G.C., Rolls, E.T., and Leonard, C.M. (1985) Selectivity between faces in the responses of a population of neurons in the cortex in the superior temporal sulcus of the monkey, *Brain Research*, **342**, 91–102.

Beaumont, J.G. (1988) *Understanding Neuropsychology*. Oxford: Blackwell.

Beehr, T.A. and Newman, J.E. (1978) Job stress, employee health, and organizational effectiveness: a facet analysis model, and literature review, *Personnel Psychology*, **31**, 665–99.

Beeman, E.A. (1947) The effect of male hormone on aggressive behaviour in mice, *Physiological Zoology*, **20**, 373–405.

Bellisle, F., Lucas, F., Amrani, R. and Le Magnen, J. (1984) Deprivation, palatability and the micro-structure of meals in human subjects, *Appetite*, **5**, 85–94.

Besson, J.M., Guilbaud, G., Abdelmoumene, M. and Chaouch, A. (1982) Physiologie de la nociception, *Journal of Physiology (Paris)*, **78**, 7–107.

Birch, A. and Hayward, S. (1994) *Individual Differences*. Basingstoke: Macmillan.

Blakemore, C. and Cooper, G.F. (1977) Development of the brain depends on the visual environment, *Nature*, **228**, 477–8.

Blanchard, E.B., Miller, S.T., Abel, G., Haynes, M. and Wicker, R. (1979) Evaluation of biofeedback in the treatment of borderline essential hypertension, *Journal of Applied Behaviour Analysis*, **12**, 99–109.

Blanchard, R.J., Fukunaga, K.K. and Blanchard, C.B. (1976) Environmental control of defensive reaction to a cat, *Bulletin of the Psychonomic Society*, **8**, 179–81.

Brala, P.M. and Hagen, R.L. (1983) Effects of sweetness perception and calorific value of a preload on short term intake, *Physiology and Behaviour*, **30**, 1–9.

Broberg, D.J. and Bernstein, I.L. (1989) Cephalic insulin release in anorexic women, *Physiology and Behaviour*, **45**, 871–4.

Broca, P. (1861) Remarques sur la siege de la faculte du langage articule, suivies d'une observation d'aphemie (perte de la parole), *Bulletin de la Societé Anatomique (Paris)*, **36**, 330–57.

Brunner, E.J., Marmot, M.G., White, I.R., O'Brien, J.R., Etherington, M.D., Slavin, B.M., Kearney, E.M. and Smith, G.D. (1993) Gender and employment grade differences in blood cholesterol, apolipoproteins and haemostatic factors in the Whitehall II study, *Atherosclerosis*, **102**(2), 195–207.

Bruyer, R., Laterre, C. and Seron, X. (1983) A case of prosopagnosia with some preserved covert remembrance of familiar faces, *Brain and Cognition*, **2**, 257–84.

Calhoun, J. (1962) Population density and social pathology, *Scientific American*, **206**, 139–48.

Campbell, N., Mackeown, W., Thomas, B. and Troscianko, T. (1995) Automatic interpretation of outdoor scenes, Paper for *British Machine Vision Conference*.

Campfield, L.A., Brandon P. and Smith, F.J. (1985) On-line continuous measurement of blood glucose and meal pattern in free-feeding rats: the role of glucose in meal imitation, *Brain Research Bulletin*, **14**, 605–617.

Cannon, W.B., (1927) The James–Lange theory of emotions: a critical examination and an alternative, *American Journal of Psychology*, **39**, 106–124.

Cannon, W.B. and Washburn, A.L. (1912) An explanation of hunger, *American Journal of Psychology*, **29**, 441–54.

Carlson, N.R. (1991) *Physiology of Behaviour*. Boston, Mass.: Allyn & Bacon.

Cloninger, C.R. (1987) Neurogenetic adaptive mechanisms in alcoholism, *Science*, **236**, 410–16.

Clugston, G.A. and Garlick, P.J. (1982) The response of protein and energy metabolism to food intake in lean and obese man, *Human Nutrition: Clinical Nutrition*, **36C**, 57–70.

Cohen, G. (1975) Cerebral apartheid: a fanciful notion?, *New Behaviour*, **18**, 458–61.

Coleman, A.M. and Beaumont, J.G. (eds) (1989) *Psychological Survey No. 7*. London: BPS/Routledge.

Conner, R.L. and Levine, S. (1969) Hormonal influences on aggressive behaviour, in S.Garattini and E.B. Sigg (eds), *Aggressive Behaviour*. New York: Wiley.

Coopersmith, S. (1968) Studies in self-esteem, *Scientific American*, **218**, 96–106.

Cottrell, G.W. and Tsung, F. (1993) Learning simple arithmetic procedures, *Connection Science*, **5**(1), 37–58.

Cox, T. and Mackay, C.J. (1976) A psychological model of occupational stress, Paper presented to the Medical Research Council meeting *Mental Health in Industry*, November, London.

Crick, F. and Mitchison, G. (1983) The function of dream sleep, *Nature*, **304**, 111–14.

Darwin, C. (1872) *Expressions of Emotion in Man and Animals.* London: John Murray.

Davies, R. (1987) Section in R.L. Gregory (ed.), *The Oxford Companion to the Mind.* Oxford: Oxford University Press.

De Castro, J.M. and de Castro, E.S. (1989) Spontaneous meal patterns of humans: influence of the presence of other people, *American Journal of Clinical Nutrition*, **50**, 237–47.

DeLongis, A., Coyne, J.C., Dakof, G., Folkman, S. and Lazarus, R.S. (1982) Relationship of daily hassles, uplifts and major life events to health status, *Health Psychology*, **1**(2), 119–36.

Dement, W. (1960) The effect of dream deprivation, *Science*, **131**, 1705–7.

Dement, W. (1972) *Some Must Watch While Some Must Sleep.* Stanford, Calif.: Stanford Alumni Association.

Dement, W. and Kleitman, N. (1957) The relation of eye-movements during sleep to dream activity: an objective method for the study of dreaming, *Journal of Experimental Psychology*, **53**(5), 339–46.

Depaulis, A., Bandler, R. and Vergnes, M. (1989) Characterisation of pretentorial periaqueductal grey matter neurons mediating intraspecific defensive behaviours in the rat by microinjections of kainic acid, *Brain Research*, **486**, 121–32.

DeValois, R.L. and DeValois, K.K. (1988) *Spatial Vision.* New York: Oxford University Press.

DeValois, R.L. and Jacobs G.H. (1984) Neural mechanisms of colour vision, in I. Dorian-Smith (ed.), *Handbook of Physiology.* Vol.3. Bethesda, Md: American Physiological Society.

Dollard, J., Doob, L.W., Miller, N.E., Mowrer, O.H. and Sears, R.R. (1939) *Frustration and Aggression.* New Haven, Conn.: Harvard University Press.

Ekman, P. (1982) *Emotion in the Human Face* (2nd edn). New York: Cambridge University Press.

Ekman, P., Levenson, R.W. and Frieson, W.V. (1983) Autonomic nervous system activity distinguishes among emotions, *Science*, **221**, 1208–10.

Empson, J. (1989) *Sleep and Dreaming.* London: Faber & Faber.

Erikson, E.H. (1980) *Identity and the Life Cycle.* New York: Norton.

Etcoff, N.L. (1985) The neuropsychology of emotional expression, in G. Goldstein and R. Tarter (eds), *Advances in Clinical Neuropsychology*, Vol.3. New York: Plenum Press.

Faraday, A. (1973) *Dream Power*. London: Pan.

Fava, M., Copeland, B.M., Schweiger, U. and Herzog, M.D. (1989) Neurochemical abnormalities of anorexia nervosa and bulimia nervosa, *American Journal of Psychiatry*, **146**, 963–71.

Floody, O.R. (1983) Hormones and aggression in female mammals, in B.B. Savare (ed.), *Hormones and Aggression*. New York: Plenum Press.

Frankenhauser, M. (1983) The sympathetic–adrenal and pituitary adrenal response to challenge: comparison between the sexes, in T.M. Dembroski, T.H. Schmidt and G. Blumchen (eds), *Behavioral Bases of Coronary Heart Disease*. Basel: S. Karger.

French, J.R.P., Caplan, R D. and Van Harrison, R. (1982) *The Mechanisms of Job Stress and Strain*. New York: Wiley.

Freud, S. (1976) *The Interpretation of Dreams*, Pelican Freud Library, Harmondsworth: Penguin (Original work published 1901).

Fried, I., Mateer, C., Ojemann, G., Wohns, R. and Fedio, P. (1982) Organisation of visuospatial functions in human cortex, *Brain*, **105**, 349–71.

Friedman, M. and Rosenman. R.H. (1974) *Type A Behaviour and Your Heart*. New York: Knopf.

Ganster, D.C. (1986) Type A behaviour and occupational stress, *Journal of Organizational Behaviour Management*, **8**(2), 61–84.

Goodall, J. (1978) Chimp killings: is it the man in them?, *Science News*, 113, 276.

Gregory, R.L. (1966) *Eye and Brain*. London: Weidenfeld & Nicolson.

Gregory, R.L. (1980) Perceptions as hypotheses, *Philosophical Transactions of the Royal Society of London, Series B*, **290**, 181–97.

Harlow, H.F., Harlow, M.K. and Meyer, D.R. (1950) Learning motivated by a manipulation drive, *Journal of Experimental Psychology*, **40**, 228–34.

Hartline, H.K. (1938) What the frog's eye tells the frog's brain, *American Journal of Physiology*, **121**, 400–6.

Hawkins, L.H. and Armstong-Esther, C.A. (1978) Circadian rhythms and night-shift working in nurses, *Nursing Times*, May 4, 49–52.

Hebb. D.O. (1950) *The Organisation of Behaviour*. New York: Wiley.

Hering, E. (1878) *Outlines of a Theory of the Light Sense* (translation) Cambridge, Mass.: Harvard University Press.

Hetherington, A.W. and Ransom, S.W. (1942) Hypothalamic lesions and adiposity in the rat, *Anatomical Record*, **78**, 149–72.

Hilgard, E.R. (1977) *Divided Consciousness: Multiple controls in human thought and action*. New York: Wiley.

Hobson, J.A. (1988) *The Dreaming Brain*. New York: Basic Books.

Hobson, J.A. and McCarley, R.W. (1977) The brain as a dream state generator: an activation–synthesis hypothesis of the dream process, *American Journal of Psychiatry*, **134**, 1335–48.

Hohmann, G.W. (1962) Some effects of spinal cord lesions on experienced emotional feelings, *Psychophysiology*, **3**, 143–56.

Holmes, T.H. and Masuda, M. (1974) Life changes and illness susceptability, in B.S. Dohrenwend and B.P. Dohrenwend (eds), *Stressful Life Events: Their nature and effects*. New York: Wiley.

Holmes, T.H. and Rahe, R.H. (1967) The Social Readjustment Rating Scale, *Journal of Psychosomatic Research*, **11**, 213–18.

Hopfield, J.J. (1984) Neural networks and physical systems with emergent collective computational properties, *Proceedings of the National Academy of Science of the USA*, **81**, 3088–92.

Horne, J. (1988) *Why We Sleep: The functions of sleep in humans and other mammals*. Oxford: Oxford University Press.

Hubel, D.H. (1977) Functional architecture of macaque monkey visual cortex, *Proceedings of the Royal Society of London, Series B*, **198**, 1–59.

Hubel, D.H. and Wiesel, T.N. (1979) Brain mechanisms of vision, *Scientific American*, **241**, 130–44.

Hughes, J., Smith, T.W., Kosterlitz, H.W., Fothergill, L.A., Morgan, B.A. and Moris, H.R. (1975) Identification of two related pentapeptides from the brain with potent opiate agonist activity, *Nature*, **258**, 577–9.

Hunter, E.J. (1979) Combat casualties who remain at home, Paper presented at Western Regional Conference of the Interuniversity Seminar *Technology in Combat*. Navy Postgraduate School, Monterey, Calif.

Hurvich, L.M. (1981) *Colour Vision*. Sunderland, Mass.: Sinauer Associates.

Jackson, S.E., Schwab, R.L. and Schuler, R.S. (1986) Toward an understanding of the burnout phenomenon, *Journal of Applied Psychology*, **71**, 630–40.

James, W. (1880) What is an emotion?, *Mind*, **9**, 188–205.

Jennett, B. (1993) Vegetative survival: the medical facts and ethical dilemmas, *Neuropsychological Rehabilitation*, 3(2), 99–108.

Jennett, B. and Plum, F. (1972) Persistent vegitative state after brain damage: a syndrome in search of a name, *Lancet*, i, 734–7.

Jermier, J.M., Gaines, J. and McIntosh, N.J. (1989) Reactions to physically dangerous work: a conceptual and empirical analysis, *Journal of Organizational Behaviour*, **10**, 15–33.

Johnson, J.H. and Sarason, I. G., (1978) Life stress, depression and anxiety: internal/external control as a moderator variable, *Journal of Psychosomatic Research*, 22(3), 205–8.

Jung, C.G. (1963) *Memories, Dreams, Reflections*. London: Collins/RKP.

Kagan, A. and Levi, L. (1975) Health and environment – psychosocial stimuli: a review, in L. Levi (ed.), *Society, Stress and Disease* Vol. 2. New York: Oxford University Press.

Kalat, J.W. (1992) *Biological Psychology* (4th edn). Belmont, Calif.: Wadsworth.

Katz, R. and Wykes, T. (1985) The psychological difference between temporally predictable and unpredictable stressful events: evidence for information control theories, *Journal of Personality and Social Psychology*, **48**, 781–90.

Keesey, R.E. and Powley, T.L. (1975) Hypothalamic regulation of body weight, *American Scientist*, **63**, 558–65.

Kihlstrom, J.F. (1984) Conscious, subconscious, unconscious: a cognitive view, in K.S. Bowers and D. Meichenbaum (eds), *The Unconscious: Reconsidered*. New York: Wiley.

Kleitman, N. (1927) Studies on the physiology of sleep, *American Journal of Physiology*, **84**, 386–95.

Kobasa, S.C. (1979) Stressful life events, personality and health: an enquiry into hardiness, *Journal of Personality and Social Psychology*, **37**, 1–11.

Kobasa, S.C., Maddi, S.R. and Kahn, S. (1982) Hardiness and health: a prospective study, *Journal of Personality and Social Psychology*, **42**, 168–77.

Laird, J.D. (1974) Self-attribution of emotion: the effects of facial expression on the quality of emotional experience, *Journal of Personality and Social Psychology*, **29**, 475–86.

Langston, J.W., Ballard, P., Tetrud, J. and Irwin, I. (1983) Chronic parkinsonism in humans due to a product of meperidine-analog synthesis, *Science*, **219**, 979–80.

Lazarus, R.S. (1966) *Psychological Stress and the Coping Process.* New York: McGraw-Hill.

Lazarus, R.S. (1976) *Patterns of Adjustment.* New York: McGraw-Hill.

Lazarus, R.S. (1982) Thoughts on the relations between emotion and cognition, *American Psychologist*, **37**, 1019–24.

Lazarus, R.S. and Folkman, S. (1984) *Stress, Appraisal and Coping.* New York: Springer.

Lazarus, R.S., Kanner, A.D. and Folkman, S. (1980) Emotions: a cognitive-phenomenological analysis, in R. Plutchik and H, Kellerman (eds), *Emotion: Theory, Research and Experience* Vol. 1. New York: Academic Press.

Ley, R.G. and Bryden, M.P. (1982) A dissociation of right and left hemispheric effects for recognising emotional tone and verbal content, *Brain and Cognition*, **1**, 3–9.

Livingstone, M.S. and Hubel, D.H. (1987) Psychophysical evidence for separate channels for the perception of form, colour, movement and depth, *Journal of Neuroscience*, **7**, 3416–68.

Lorenz, K.Z. (1966) *On Aggression.* London: Methuen.

Louis-Sylvestre, J. and Le Magnen, J. (1980) A fall in blood-glucose levels precedes meal onset in free-feeding rats, *Neuroscience and Biobehavioural Reviews*, **4**, 13–16.

Mackay, D. (1987) Divided brains – divided minds?, in C. Blakemore and S. Greenfield (eds), *Mindwaves.* Oxford: Blackwell.

McFarland, D.J. (1971) *Feedback Mechanisms in Animal Behaviour.* New York: Academic Press.

Maksay, G. and Ticku, M.K. (1985) Dissociation of [35S] t-butylbicyclophosphorothionate binding differentiates convulsant and depressant drugs that modulate GABAergic transmission, *Journal of Neurochemistry*, **44**, 480–6.

Malim, T. (1994) *Cognitive Processes.* Basingstoke: Macmillan.

Malim, T., Birch, A. and Hayward, S. (1996) *Comparative Psychology: A sociobiological approach.* Basingstoke: Macmillan.

Malim, T., Birch, A. and Wadeley, A. (1992) *Perspectives in Psychology.* Basingstoke: Macmillan.

Mandler, G. (1982) *Mind and Emotion.* New York: Norton.

Maslach, C. (1979) Negative emotional biasing of unexplained arousal, *Journal of Personality and Social Psychology*, **37**, 953–69.

Maslach, C. and Jackson, S.E. (1981) The measurement of experienced burnout, *Journal of Occupational Behaviour*, **2**, 99–113.

Maslow, A. (1970) *Motivation and Personality*, New York: Harper & Row.

Matthews, T. (1988) The association of Type A behaviour with cardiovascular disease: update and critical review, in B. Kent Houston and G.R. Snyder (eds), *Type A Behaviour Pattern: Research, Theory and Intervention*. New York: Wiley.

Meddis, R. (1983) The evolution of sleep, in A. Mayes (ed), *Sleep Mechanisms and Functions*. London: Van Nostrand Reinholt.

Meijer, J. H. and Reitveld, W.J. (1989) Neurophysiology of the suprachiasmatic circadian pacemaker in rodents, *Physiological Reviews*, **69**, 671–707.

Miles, L.E., Raynan, D.M. and Wilson, M.A. (1977) Blind man living in normal society has circadian rhythm of 24.9 hours, *Science*, **198**, 421–3.

Morris, D. (1982) *Manwatching*. London: Triad/Granada.

Norman, D.A. (1993) Twelve issues for cognitive science, in A.M. Aitkenhead and J.M. Slack, *Issues in Cognitive Modelling*. London: Lawrence Erlbaum/OU.

Numan, M. (1974) Medial preoptic area and maternal behaviour in the female rat, *Journal of Comparative and Physiological Psychology*, **87**, 746–59.

Olds, J. and Milner, P. (1954) Positive reinforcement produced by electrical stimulation of septal area and other regions of the rat brain, *Journal of Comparative and Physiological Psychology*, **47**, 419–27.

Orne, M.T. (1979) On the simulating subject as quasi-control group in hypnosis research: what, why and how?, in E. Fromm and R.E. Shor (eds), *Hypnosis: Research developments and perspectives*. New York: Aldine.

Ornstein, R. (1986) *The Psychology of Consciousness* (2nd edn). Harmondsworth: Penguin.

Oswald, I. (1980) Sleep as a restorative process: human clues, *Process in Brain Research*, **53**, 279–88.

Patton, G. (1989) The course of anorexia nervosa, *British Medical Journal*, **299**, 139–40.

Pert, C.B., Snowman, A.M. and Snyder, S.H. (1974) Localisation of opiate receptor binding in presynaptic membranes of rat brain, *Brain Research*, **70**, 184–8.

Pilleri, G. (1979) The blind Indus dolphin, *Endeavours*, **3**, 48–56.

Plutchik, R. (1980) A general psychoevolutionary theory of emotion, in R. Plutchik and H. Kellerman (eds), *Emotion: Theory, Research and Experience* Vol.1. New York: Academic Press.

Rahe, R.H. and Arthur, R.J. (1977) Life change patterns surrounding illness experience, in A. Monat and R.S. Lazarus (eds), *Stress and Coping*. New York: Columbia University Press.

Rodin, J., Schank, D. and Striegel-Moore, R. (1989) Psychological features of obesity, *Medical Clinics of North America*, **73**, 47–66.

Rolls, B.J., Rowe, E.A., Rolls, E.T., Kingston, B., Megson, A. and Gunary, R. (1981) Variety in a meal enhances food intake in man, *Physiology and Behaviour*, **26**, 215–21.

Rolls, E.T., Baylis, G.C., Hasselmo, M.E. and Nalwa, V. (1989) The effect of learning on the face selective responses of neurons in the cortex in the superior temporal sulculus of monkeys, *Experimental Brain Research*, **76**, 153–64.

Rose, S. (1976) *The Conscious Brain*. Harmondsworth: Penguin.

Rotter, J.B. (1966) Generalised expectancies for internal versus external control of reinforcement, *Psychological Monographs*, **30**(1), 1–26.

Russek, M. (1971) Hepatic receptors and the neurophysiological mechanisms controlling feeding behaviour, in S. Ehrenpreis (ed.), *Neurosciences research* Vol.4. New York: Academic Press.

Sachs, B.D. and Meisel, R.L. (1988) The physiology of male sexual behaviour, in E. Knobil and J. Neill (eds), *The Physiology of Reproduction*. New York: Raven Press.

Schachter, S. (1964) The interaction of cognitive and physiological determinants of emotional state, in L. Berkowitz (ed.), *Advances in Experimental Social Psychology*, Vol.1. New York: Academic Press.

Schacter, S. and Singer, J.E. (1962) Cognitive, social and physiological determinants of emotional state, *Psychological Review*, **69**, 379–99.

Schleifer, S.J., Keller, S.E., McKegney, F.P. and Stein, M. (1979) The influence of stress and other psychosocial factors on human immunity, Paper presented at the 36th Annual Meeting of the Psychosomatic Society, Dallas, March 1979.

Seligman, M.E.P. (1975) *Helplessness: On depression, development and death*. San Francisco: W.H. Freeman.

Selye, H. (1956) *The Stress of Life*. New York: McGraw-Hill.

Shimizu, N., Oomura, Y., Novin, D., Grijalva, C and Cooper, P.H. (1983) Functional correlations between lateral hypothalamic glucose-sensitive neurons and hepatic portal glucose-sensitive units in rats, *Brain Research*, **265**, 49–54.

Smuts, B.B., Cheney, D.L., Seyfarth, R., Wrangham, R. and Struhsaker, T.T. (eds) (1987) *Primate Societies*. Chicago: University of Chicago Press.

Speisman, J.C., Lazarus, R.S., Mordkoff, A.M. and Davidson, L.A. (1964) The experimental reduction of stress based on ego defence theory, *Journal of Abnormal and Social Psychology*, **68**, 397–8.

Sperry, R.W. (1968) Hemisphere deconnection and unity in conscious awareness, *American Psychologist*, **23**, 723–33.

Squire, L.R. (1986) Mechanisms of memory, *Science*, **232**, 1612–19.

Stunkard, A.J., Sorensen, T.I.A., Harris, C., Teasdale, T.W., Chakraborty, R., Schull, W.J. and Schulsinger, F. (1986) An adoption study of human obesity, *New England Journal of Medicine*, **314**, 193–8.

Sugden, D., Vanacek, J., Klein, D., Thomas, T. and Anderson, W. (1985) Activation of protein kinase C potentiates isoprenaline-included cyclic AMP accummulation in rat pinealocytes, *Nature*, **314**, 359–62.

Svaetichin, G. (1956) Spectral response curves from single cones, *Acta Physiologica Scandinavica*, **39**(Suppl. 134), 17–46.

Tanabe, T., Iino, M., Ooshima, Y. and Tagaki, S.F. (1974) An olfactory area in the prefrontal lobe, *Brain Research*, **80**, 127–30.

Van de Pompe, G. and de Heus, P. (1993) Work stress, social support and strains among male and female managers, *Anxiety, Stress and Coping: An International Journal*, **6**(3), 215–29.

Von Bekesy, G. (1960) *Experiments in Hearing*. New York: McGraw-Hill.

Vor Helmholtz, H.L.F. (1885) *Sensations of Tone*. London: Longmans.

Webb, W.B. (1982) Some theories about sleep and their clinical implications, *Psychiatric Annals*, **11**, 415–22.

Weiner, B. (1985) An attributional theory of achievement motivation and emotion, *Psychological Review*, **92**, 548–73.

Weiskrantz, L. (1987) Residual vision in a scotoma: a follow-up study of 'form' discrimination, *Brain*, **110**, 77–92.

Weiskrantz, L., Warrington, E.K., Sanders, M.D. and Marshall, J. (1974) Visual capacity in the hemianopic field following a restricted occipital ablation, *Brain*, **97**, 709–28.

Wilson, E.O. (1983) Statement cited in 'Mother nature's murderers', *Discovery*, October, 79–82.

Wolfgang, A.P. (1988) Job stress in the health professionals: a study of physicians, nurses and pharmacists, *Behavioral Medicine*, **14**, 43–7.

Yamamoto, T., Yuyama, N. and Kawamura, Y. (1981) Central processing of taste perception, in Y. Katsuki, R. Norgren and M. Sato (eds), *Brain Mechanisms of Sensation*. New York: Wiley.

Index